ASTROLOGY AND RELIGION

among the Greeks and Romans

by FRANZ CUMONT

DOVER PUBLICATIONS, INC.
New York

MAURITIO JASTROW

BABYLONIORUM

ASTROLOGIAE

INTERPRETI SAGACISSIMO

Published in Canada by General Publishing Company, Ltd., 30 Lesmill Road, Don Mills, Toronto, Ontario.

Published in the United Kingdom by Constable and Company, Ltd., 10 Orange Street, London WC 2.

This Dover edition, first published in 1960, is an unabridged and unaltered republication of the work originally published in 1912 by G. P. Putnam's Sons.

International Standard Book Number: 0-486-20581-9

Library of Congress Catalog Card Number: 60-50835

Manufactured in the United States of America
Dover Publications, Inc.
180 Varick Street
New York, N. Y. 10014

PREFACE

It is the purpose of these lectures delivered under the auspices of the American Committee for Lectures on the History of Religions, to sum up the results of researches carried on by me for many years in the field of ancient astrology and astral religion. For some facts set forth here in a summary fashion, I can refer the reader interested in the details to a number of special articles published in various periodicals; the proof of other assertions will be given in a larger work that I hope at some future date to publish on this same general theme.

My sincere thanks are due to Mr. J. B. Baker of Oxford who has carried out the task of translating these lectures in so satisfactory a manner; and I am also largely indebted to my friend, Mr. J. G. C. Anderson of Christ Church, who was kind enough to undertake the revision of the manuscript. I also owe some valuable corrections to Prof. Morris Jastrow, Jr., of the University of Pennsylvania, who, as Secretary of the American Committee, may be said to have called this book into existence, and to whom I take pleasure in dedicating the volume, as a mark of recognition of his own researches in the cognate field of Babylonian-Assyrian astrology.

Brussels,   FRANZ CUMONT
January, 1912

CONTENTS

ANNOUNCEMENT

The American Lectures on the History of Religions are delivered under the auspices of the American Committee for Lectures on the History of Religions. This Committee was organised in 1892, for the purpose of instituting "popular courses in the History of Religions, somewhat after the style of the Hibbert Lectures in England, to be delivered by the best scholars of Europe and this country, in various cities, such as Baltimore, Boston, Brooklyn, Chicago, New York, Philadelphia, and others."

The terms of association under which the Committee exists are as follows:

1.—The object of this Association shall be to provide courses of lectures on the history of religions, to be delivered in various cities.

2.—The Association shall be composed of delegates from the institutions agreeing to co-operate, with such additional members as may be chosen by these delegates.

3.—These delegates—one from each institution, with the additional members selected—shall constitute themselves a Council under the name of the "American Committee for Lectures on the History of Religions."

4.—The Council shall elect out of its number a Chairman, a Secretary, and a Treasurer.

5.—All matters of local detail shall be left to the co-operating institution under whose auspices the lectures are to be delivered.

6.—A course of lectures on some religion, or phase of religion, from an historical point of view, or on a subject germane to the study of religions, shall be delivered annually, or at such intervals as may be found practicable, in the different cities represented by this Association.

7.—The Council (a) shall be charged with the selection of the lecturers, (b) shall have charge of the funds, (c) shall assign the time for the lectures in each city, and perform such other functions as may be necessary.

8.—Polemical subjects, as well as polemics in the treatment of subjects, shall be positively excluded.

9.—The lectures shall be delivered in the various cities between the months of September and June.

10.—The copyright of the lectures shall be the property of the Association.

11.—The compensation of the lecturer shall be fixed in each case by the Council.

12.—The lecturer shall be paid in instalments after each course, until he shall have received half of the entire compensation. Of the remaining half, one half shall be paid to him upon delivery of the manuscript, properly prepared for the press, and the second half on the publication of the volume, less a deduction for corrections made by the author in the proofs.

The Committee as now constituted is as follows:

Prof. Crawford H. Toy, Chairman, 7 Lowell St., Cambridge, Mass.; Rev. Dr. John P. Peters, Treasurer, 227 W. 99th St., New York City; Prof. Morris Jastrow, Jr., Secretary, 248 S. 23rd St., Philadelphia, Pa.; President Francis Brown, Union Theological Seminary, New York City; Prof. Richard Gottheil, Columbia University, New York City; Prof. Robert F. Harper, University of Chicago, Chicago, Ill.; Prof. Paul Haupt, Johns Hopkins University, Baltimore, Md.; Prof. F. W. Hooper, Brooklyn Institute of Arts and Sciences; Prof. E. W. Hopkins, Yale University, New Haven, Conn.; Prof. Edward Knox Mitchell, Hartford Theological Seminary, Hartford, Conn.; President F. K. Sanders, Washburn College, Topeka, Kan.; Prof. H. P. Smith, Meadville Theological Seminary, Meadville, Pa.

The lecturers in the course of American Lectures on the History of Religions and the titles of their volumes are as follows:

1894–1895—Prof. T. W. Rhys-Davids, Ph.D.—Buddhism.

1896–1897—Prof. Daniel G. Brinton, M.D., LL.D.—Religions of Primitive Peoples.

1897–1898—Rev. Prof. T. K. Cheyne, D.D.—Jewish Religious
Life after the Exile.

1898–1899—Prof. Karl Budde, D.D.—Religion of Israel to the
Exile.

1904–1905—Prof. George Steindorff, Ph.D.—The Religion of
the Ancient Egyptians.

1905–1906—Prof. George W. Knox, D.D., LL.D.—The
Development of Religion in Japan.

1906–1907—Prof. Maurice Bloomfield, Ph.D., LL.D.—The
Religion of the Veda.

1907–1908—Prof. A. V. W. Jackson, Ph.D., LL.D.—The
Religion of Persia.[1]

1909–1910—Prof. Morris Jastrow, Jr., Ph.D.—Aspects of
Religious Belief and Practice in Babylonia and
Assyria.

1910–1911—Prof. J. J. M. DeGroot.—The Development of
Religion in China.

The lecturer for 1911–1912 was Prof. Franz Cumont of
Brussels, recognised as the leading authority on Greek Astrology and Mithraism. From 1892 until his resignation in 1910,
Prof. Cumont held the Chair of Roman Institutions at the
University of Ghent. Since 1899, he has been Curator of the
Royal Museums of Antiquities at Brussels. Prof. Cumont's great
work on the Mithra Cult was published in 1894–1900, and is
the standard work on that subject. This was followed by a
smaller summary, *Les Mystères de Mithra*, of which an English
translation, under the title "Mysteries of Mithra," was published in 1903. A series of lectures delivered at the Collège de
France on *Les Religions Orientales dans le Paganisme Romain*

[1] This course was not published by the Committee, but will form part of Prof.
Jackson's volume on the Religion of Persia in the series of "Handbooks on the
History of Religions," edited by Prof. Morris Jastrow, Jr., and published by
Messrs. Ginn & Company of Boston. Prof. Jastrow's volume is, therefore, the
eighth in the series. Prof. De Groot's lectures have not yet been published, but will
appear in 1912. Prof. Cumont's volume is, therefore, the ninth in the series.

(Paris, 1907; 2nd ed. 1910) has also appeared in an English garb (Oriental Religions in Roman Paganism. Chicago, 1911).

In 1900 and again in 1907, Prof. Cumont conducted archæological explorations in Asia Minor and in Northern Syria, the results of which were embodied in his *Studia Pontica* (Brussels, 1906) and in a volume of Greek and Latin inscriptions published in 1911.

In 1898, in collaboration with several scholars, M. Cumont undertook a catalogue, with detailed descriptions and copious extracts, of all Greek astrological codices (*Catalogus Codicum Astrologorum Graecorum*), of which monumental work, up to the present, ten volumes have appeared. A Bibliography of Prof. Cumont's writings, including numerous articles contributed by him to archæological, historical, and philosophical journals of various countries, was published in 1908 by the Royal Academy of Belgium, of which body M. Cumont has been a member since 1902. He is also a corresponding member of the Institute de France and of the Academies of Berlin, Göttingen, and Munich.

The lectures contained in this volume are a summary in a popular form of extensive researches carried on by Prof. Cumont for many years. They were delivered before the following institutions: The Lowell Institute, Hartford Theological Seminary, Johns Hopkins University, University of Pennsylvania, University of Chicago, Brooklyn Institute of Arts and Sciences, Meadville Theological Seminary, and Columbia University.

JOHN P. PETERS,
C. H. TOY,
Committee on Publication

December, 1911

INTRODUCTION

*'Εκ τῶν οὐρανίων τὰ ἐπίγεια ἤρτηται
κατά τινα φυσικὴν συμπάθειαν.*

PHILO, *De Opificio Mundi*, c. 40.

After a long period of discredit and neglect, astrology is
beginning to force itself once more on the attention of the
learned world. In the course of the last few years scholars have
devoted to it profound researches and elaborate publications.
Greek manuscripts, which had remained a sealed book at a
time when the quest for unpublished documents is all the rage,
have now been laboriously examined, and the wealth of this
literature has exceeded all expectation. On the other hand, the
deciphering of the cuneiform tablets has given access to the well-
springs of a learned superstition, which up to modern times has
exercised over Asia and Europe a wider dominion than any
religion has ever achieved. I trust, therefore, that I am not
guilty of undue presumption in venturing to claim your
interest for this erroneous belief, so long universally accepted,
which exercised an endless influence on the creeds and the
ideas of the most diverse peoples, and which for that very
reason necessarily demands the attention of historians.

After a duration of a thousand years, the power of astrology
broke down when, with Copernicus, Kepler, and Galileo, the
progress of astronomy overthrew the false hypothesis upon
which its entire structure rested, namely, the geocentric
system of the universe. The fact that the earth revolves in space
intervened to upset the complicated play of planetary influences, and the silent stars, relegated to the unfathomable
depths of the sky, no longer made their prophetic voices
audible to mankind. Celestial mechanics and spectrum
analysis finally robbed them of their mysterious prestige.
Thenceforth in that learned system of divination, which professed to discover from the stars the secret of our destiny, men
saw nothing but the most monstrous of all the chimeras be-
gotten of superstition. Under the sway of reason the eighteenth

and nineteenth centuries condemned this heresy in the name of
scientific orthodoxy. In 1824, Letronne thought it necessary to
apologise for discoursing to the Academy of Inscriptions on
"absurd dreams" in which he saw "nothing but one of those
failings which have done most dishonour to the human mind," [1]
—as though man's failings were not often more instructive
than his triumphs.

But at the end of the nineteenth century the development of
history, from various sides, recalled the attention of investigators
to ancient astrology. It is an exact science which was super-
imposed on primitive beliefs, and when classical philology,
enlarging its horizon, brought fully within its range of observation the development of the sciences in antiquity, it could not
set aside a branch of knowledge, illegitimate, I allow, but in-
dissolubly linked not only with astronomy and meteorology,
but also with medicine, botany, ethnography, and physics. If
we go back to the earliest stages of every kind of learning, as
far as the Alexandrine and even the Babylonian period, we
shall find almost everywhere the disturbing influence of these
astral "mathematics." This sapling, which shot up among the
rank weeds by the side of the tree of knowledge, sprang from
the same stock and mingled its branches with it.

But not only is astrology indispensable to the *savant* who
desires to trace the toilsome progress of reason in the pursuit of
truth along its doublings and turnings,—which is perhaps the
highest mission of history; it also benefited by the interest
which was roused in all manifestations of the irrational. This
pseudo-science is in reality a creed. Beneath the icy crust of a
cold and rigid dogma run the troubled waters of a jumble of
worships, derived from an immense antiquity; and as soon as
enquiry was directed to the religions of the past, it was attracted
to this doctrinal superstition, perhaps the most astonishing that
has ever existed. Research ascertained how, after having
reigned supreme in Babylonia, it subdued the cults of Syria and
of Egypt, and under the Empire,—to mention only the West,—
transformed even the ancient paganism of Greece and Rome.

It is not only, however, because it is combined with scientific

---

[1] "*Rêveries absurdes . . . une des faiblesses qui ont le plus déshonoré l'esprit humain.*"

theories, nor because it enters into the teaching of pagan mysteries, that astrology forces itself on the meditations of the historian of religions, but for its own sake (and here we touch the heart of the problem), because he is obliged to enquire how and why this alliance, which at first sight seems monstrous, came to be formed between mathematics and superstition. It is no explanation to consider it merely a mental disease. Even then, to speak the truth, this hallucination, the most persistent which has ever haunted the human brain, would still deserve to be studied. If psychology to-day conscientiously applies itself to disorders of the memory and of the will, it cannot fail to interest itself in the ailments of the faculty of belief, and specialists in lunacy will do useful work in dealing with this species of morbid manifestation with the view of settling its etiology and tracing its course. How could this absurd doctrine arise, develop, spread, and force itself on superior intellects for century after century? There, in all its simplicity, is the historical problem which confronts us.

In reality the growth of this body of dogma followed a course not identical with, but parallel, I think, to that of certain other theologies. Its starting-point was faith, faith in certain stellar divinities who exerted an influence on the world. Next, people sought to comprehend the nature of this influence: they believed it to be subject to certain invariable laws, because observation revealed the fact that the heavens were animated by regular movements, and they conceived themselves able to determine its effects in the future with the same certainty as the coming revolutions and conjunctions of the stars. Finally, when a series of theories had been evolved out of that twofold conviction, their original source was forgotten or disregarded. The old belief became a science; its postulates were erected into principles, which were justified by physical and moral reasons, and it was pretended that they rested on experimental data amassed by a long series of observations. By a common process, after believing, people invented reasons for believing,—"*fides quaerens intellectum*,"—and the intelligence working on the faith reduced it to formulæ, the logical sequence of which concealed the radical fallacy.

There is something tragic in this ceaseless attempt of man to penetrate the mysteries of the future, in this obstinate struggle of his faculties to lay hold on knowledge which evades his probe, and to satisfy his insatiable desire to foresee his destiny. The birth and evolution of astrology, that desperate error on which the intellectual powers of countless generations were spent, seems like the bitterest of disillusions. By establishing the un-changeable character of the celestial revolutions the Chaldeans imagined that they understood the mechanism of the universe, and had discovered the actual laws of life. The ancient beliefs in the influence of the stars upon the earth were concentrated into dogmas of absolute rigidity. But these dogmas were fre-quently contradicted by experience, which ought to have con-firmed them. Then not daring to doubt the principles on which depended their whole conception of the world, these soothsayer-logicians strove to correct their theories. Unable to bring themselves to deny the influence of the divine stars on the affairs of this world, they invented new methods for the better determination of this influence, they complicated by irrelevant data the problem, of which the solution had proved false, and thus there was piled up little by little in the course of ages a monstrous collection of complicated and often contradictory doctrines, which perplex the reason, and whose audacious un-substantiality will remain a perpetual subject of astonishment. We should be confounded at the spectacle of the human mind losing itself so long in the maze of these errors, did we not know how medicine, physics, and chemistry have slowly groped their way before becoming experimental sciences, and what prolonged exertions they have had to make in order to free themselves from the tenacious grasp of old superstitions.

Thus various reasons commended to the attention of scholars these old writings of the Greek astrologers so long neglected. They set to work to re-read and to re-publish these repulsive-looking books which had not been reprinted since the sixteenth century. The last edition—and a shockingly bad one—of the *Tetrabiblos* of Ptolemy is dated 1581. Further, a number of unknown authors emerged from obscurity, a crowd of manuscripts mouldering in the tombs of libraries were restored to light.[1]

The profit which can be gained from them is not confined to the science of which they treat and to the adjacent domains, which astrology has more or less penetrated. Their utility is much more varied and general, and it would be difficult to set out in full their manifold applications.[2]

I shall not dwell on the interest afforded to the scholar by a series of texts spread over more than fifteen centuries, from the Alexandrine period to the Renaissance. Nor, again, will I attempt to estimate the importance which might be claimed in the political sphere by a doctrine which has often guided the will of kings, and decided their enterprises. Nor can I prove here by examples how the propagation of astrological doctrines reveals unsuspected relations between the oldest civilisations, and leads him who traces it from Alexandria and from Babylon as far as India, China, and Japan, bringing him back again from the Far East to the Far West.

So many questions of such varied interest cannot be considered all at once. We must exercise restraint and confine ourselves to one view of the subject. Our object in this course of lectures shall be limited to showing how oriental astrology and star-worship transformed the beliefs of the Græco-Latin world, what at different periods was the ever-increasing strength of their influence, and by what means they established in the West a sidereal cult, which was the highest phase of ancient paganism. In Greek anthropomorphism the Olympians were merely an idealised reflection of various human personalities. Roman formalism made the worship of the national gods an expression of patriotism, strictly regulated by pontifical and civil law. Babylon was the first to erect the edifice of a *cosmic* religion, based upon science, which brought human activity and human relations with the astral divinities into the

---

[1] See *Catalogus Codicum Astrologorum Graecorum* (ten volumes published), Brussels, 1893–1911.

[2] See Franz Boll, *Zur Erforschung der antiken Astrologie* (Neue Jahrbücher f. d. Klass. Altertum), xxi (1903).

general harmony of organised nature. This learned theology, by including in its speculations the entire world, was to eliminate the narrower forms of belief, and, by changing the character of ancient idolatry, it was to prepare in many respects the coming of Christianity.

LECTURE I. *The Chaldeans*

During the period of the French Revolution citizen Dupuis, in three bulky volumes "On the Origin of all Forms of Worship" (1794), developed the idea that the primary source of religion was the spectacle of celestial phenomena and the ascertainment of their correspondence with earthly events, and he undertook to show that the myths of all peoples and all times were nothing but a set of astronomical combinations. According to him, the Egyptians, to whom he assigned the foremost place among "the inventors of religions," had conceived, some twelve or fifteen thousand years before our era, the division of the ecliptic into twelve constellations corresponding to the twelve months; and when the expedition of Bonaparte discovered in the temples of the Nile valley, notably at Denderah, some zodiacs to which a fabulous antiquity was attributed, these extraordinary theories appeared to receive an unexpected confirmation. But the bold mythological fabric reared in the heavens by the *savant* of the Revolution fell to pieces when Letronne proved that the zodiac of Denderah dated, not from an epoch anterior to the most ancient of the known Pharaohs, but from that of the Roman emperors.

Science in her cycles of hypotheses is liable to repeat herself. An attempt has recently been made to restore to favour the fancies of Dupuis, by renovating them with greater erudition. Only, the mother country of "astral mythology" is to be sought, not on the banks of the Nile, but on those of the Euphrates. The "Pan-Babylonists," as they have been called, maintain that

Behind the literature and cults of Babylon and Assyria, behind the legends and myths, behind the Pantheon and religious beliefs, behind even the writings which appear to be purely historical, lies an astral conception of the universe and of its phenomena, affecting all thoughts, all beliefs, all practices, and penetrating even into the

3

domain of purely secular intellectual activity, including all branches of science cultivated in antiquity. According to this astral conception, the greater gods were identified with the planets, and the minor ones with the fixed stars. A scheme of correspondences between phenomena in the heavens and occurrences on earth was worked out. The constantly changing appearance of the heavens indicates the ceaseless activity of the gods, and since whatever happened on earth was due to divine powers, this activity represented the preparation for terrestrial phenomena, and more particularly those affecting the fortunes of mankind. . . . Proceeding further, it is claimed that the astral-mythological cult of ancient Babylonia became the prevailing *Weltanschauung* of the ancient Orient, and that whether we turn to Egypt or to Palestine, to Hittite districts or to Arabia, we shall find these various cultures under the spell of this conception.

It furnishes the key to the interpretation of Homer as well as of the Bible.[1] In particular, all the Old Testament should be explained by a series of sidereal myths. The patriarchs are "personifications of the sun or moon," and the traditions of the Sacred Books are "variations of certain 'motifs,' whose real significance is to be found only when they are transferred to phenomena in the heavens."

Such is a wholly impartial summary of the theories professed by the advocates of the *Altorientalische Weltanschauung*. I borrow it, with slight abbreviation, from an address delivered by Morris Jastrow, Jr., at the Oxford Congress in 1908.[2] Now of this system it may be said that what is true in it is not new, and what is new is not true. That Babylon was the mother of astronomy, star-worship, and astrology, that thence these sciences and these beliefs spread over the world, is a fact already told us by the ancients, and the course of these lectures will prove it clearly. But the mistake of the Pan-Babylonists, whose wide generalisations rest on the narrowest and flimsiest of bases, lies in the fact that they have transferred to the nebulous origins of history conceptions which were not developed at the beginning but quite at the end of Babylonian civilisation. This

---

[1] See e.g. Fries, *Studien zur Odyssee* (Mitt. Vorderasiat. Gesellschaft), 1910.
[2] *Transactions of the Third International Congress for the History of Religions*. Oxford, 1908, i, p. 234; cf. Jastrow, *Die Religion Babyloniens und Assyriens*, ii (1910), p. 432.

vast theology, founded upon the observation of the stars, which is assumed to have been built up thousands of years before our era,—nay, before the Trojan War,—and to have imposed itself on all still barbarous peoples as the expression of a mysterious wisdom, cannot have been in existence at this remote period, for the simple reason that the data on which it would have been founded, were as yet unknown.

How often, for instance, has the theory of the precession of the equinoxes been brought into the religious cosmology of the East ! But what becomes of all these symbolical explanations, if the fact be established that the Orientals never had a suspicion of this famous precession before the genius of Hipparchus discovered it ?[1] Just as the dreams of Dupuis vanished when the date of the Egyptian zodiacs was settled, so the Babylonian mirage was dispelled when scholars advanced methodically through the desert of cuneiform inscriptions and determined the date when astronomy began to take shape, as an exact science, in the observatories of Mesopotamia. This new delusion will depart to the realm of dreams to join the idea, so dear to poets of old, of Chaldean shepherds discovering the causes of eclipses while watching their flocks.

When we have to ascertain at what date oriental star-worship effected the transformation of Syrian and Greek paganism, we shall not find it necessary to plunge into the obscurity of the earliest times; we shall be able to study the facts in the full light of history. "An astral theory of the universe is not an outcome of popular thought, but the result of a long process of speculative reasoning carried on in restricted learned circles. Even astrology, which the theory presupposes as a foundation, is not a product of primitive popular fancies but is rather an advanced scientific hypothesis."[2] In this first lecture, then, we shall have to begin by asking ourselves at what date a scientific astronomy and astrology were developed at Babylon, and then proceed to examine how they led to the formation of

---

[1] See below, Lecture II, p. 34.

[2] Jastrow, *l. c.*, p. 236.—Since this lecture was written, an excellent paper on this subject has been published by Carl Bezold, *Astronomie, Himmelschau und Astrallehre bei den Babyloniern* (Sitzungsb. Akad. Heidelberg, 1911, Abh. No. 2).

a learned theology and gave to Babylonian religion its ultimate character.

⚜   ⚜

Let us consult, the historians of astronomy. The original documents of Chaldean erudition have been deciphered and published during these last twenty years mainly by the industry of Strassmaier and Kugler,[1] and we are able to-day to realise to some extent what knowledge the Babylonians possessed at different periods.

Now here is one first discovery pregnant with consequences: before the eighth century no scientific astronomy was possible owing to the absence of one indispensable condition, namely, the possession of an exact system of chronology. The old calendar already in use about the year 2500, and perhaps earlier, was composed of twelve lunar months. But as twelve lunar periods make only 354 days, a thirteenth month was from time to time inserted to bring the date at which the festivals recurred each year, into harmony with the seasons. It was only little by little that greater precision was attained by observing at what date the heliac rising of certain fixed stars took place. So inaccurate a computation of time allowed of no precise calculations and consequently of no astronomy worthy of the name. In fact, during the first twenty or thirty centuries of Mesopotamian history nothing is found but empirical observations, intended chiefly to indicate omens, and the rudimentary knowledge which these observations display, is hardly in advance of that of the Egyptians, the Chinese, or the Aztecs. These early observers could employ only such methods as do not necessitate the record of periodic phenomena. For instance, the determination of the four cardinal points by means of the rising and setting of the sun, for use in the orientation of temples, was known from the very earliest antiquity.

But by degrees, direct observation of celestial phenomena, intended either to enable soothsayers to make predictions or to fix the calendar, led to the establishment of the fact that certain

[1] F. X. Kugler, S. J., *Die Babylonische Mondrechnung*, 1900, and *Sternkunde und Sterndienst in Babel*, 1907–1909 (in progress). A clear and able résumé of Kugler's researches has been given by Schiaparelli; see below, p. 13.

of these phenomena recurred at regular intervals, and the attempt was then made to base predictions on the calculation of this recurrence or periodicity. This necessitated a strict chronology, at which the Babylonians did not arrive till the middle of the eighth century B.C.: in 747 they adopted the so-called "era of Nabonassar." This was not a political or religious era, or one signalised by any important event. It merely indicated the moment when, doubtless owing to the establishment of a lunisolar cycle, they kept properly constructed chronological tables. Farther back there was no certainty in regard to the calculation of time. It is from that moment that the records of eclipses begin which Ptolemy used, and which are still sometimes employed by men of science for the purpose of testing their lunar theories. The oldest is dated March 21, 721 B.C.[1]

For the period of the Sargonides, who reigned over Nineveh from the year 722, the documents of the famous library of Ashurbanapal, and especially the reports made to these Assyrian kings by the official astrologers, allow us to form a sufficiently clear idea of the state of their astronomical knowledge. They had approximately traced the ecliptic, that is, the line which the sun seems to follow in the sky during its annual course, and they had divided it into four parts corresponding to the four seasons. Without having succeeded in establishing the real zodiac, they attempted at any rate, with the object of testing the calendar, to draw up the list of constellations whose heliac rising corresponded to the various months. From the fixed stars they already distinguished the planets to the number of five; they had traced their course, now forwards now backwards, and determined, at least approximately, the duration of their synodic revolutions,—for instance, one tablet calculates that this duration in the case of Venus is 577.5 days, instead of the actual 584. But as yet they had no idea of their respective distances from the earth, for the order in which the seven principal stars are enumerated in the inscriptions of Nineveh,—the Moon, the Sun, Jupiter, Venus, Saturn, Mercury, Mars,

---

[1] One of these eclipses is noted both in Ptolemy's *Almagest* and in a cuneiform tablet, see Boll, in Pauly-Wissowa's *Realencyclopädie*, s. v. "Finsternisse," col. 2354.

—has no relation to any astronomical fact. Jupiter, or Marduk, is put at the head of the five planets, because Marduk is the principal god of Babylon. Finally, those priests had not only fixed with remarkable accuracy the duration of the lunar period at a little more than twenty-nine and one half days, but, having ascertained that eclipses occurred with a certain periodicity, they had gone so far as frequently—but not regularly—to predict their recurrence. In their reports to the kings of Nineveh astrologers often prided themselves on the fact that an eclipse which they had foreseen, had occurred. This was their great achievement.

The destruction of Nineveh in the year 606 B.C. did not interrupt the conquests of astronomy. Under Nebuchadnezzar (604–561) Babylon returned to the days of her past glory, and in this ancient sanctuary of science, amid the general prosperity, astronomy received a new impetus, which was not checked by the almost voluntary submission of the old Semitic capital to the kings of Persia in 539. A valuable tablet, dated 523, shows the astonishing advance made since the fall of Assyria. Here for the first time we find the relative positions of the sun and the moon calculated in advance; we find, noted with their precise dates, the conjunctions of the moon with the planets and of the planets with each other, and their situation in the signs of the zodiac, which here appears definitely established,—or, to put it more briefly, the monthly ephemerides of the sun and the moon, the principal phenomena of the planets, and eclipses. All this indicates an intensity of thought and a perseverance in observation of which we have as yet no other example, and F. X. Kugler has therefore very properly regarded this tablet as the oldest known document of the *scientific* astronomy of the Chaldeans. True science is at length disencumbered of the empirical determinations which had accumulated in the course of many centuries. From that time some fifty documents, now deciphered,—the most recent of which belongs to the year 8 B.C.,—enable us to follow its development under the dominion of the Persians, the Macedonians, and the Parthians until about the commencement of our era. There is noticeable a continual advance and an increasing improvement in the methods employed, at least up to the end of the second century B.C., to which belong the most perfect examples which we possess. Chronological reckonings are rendered more accurate by the adoption of a lunisolar cycle of nineteen years; the zodiac is definitely established by the substitution for the ancient constellations of variable sizes of a geometrical division of the circle in which the planets move, into twelve equal parts, each subdivided into three portions or decans, equivalent to ten of our degrees. If the Babylonians were not aware of the precession of the equinoxes before the Greeks, at least they discovered the inequality of the seasons, resulting from a variation in the apparent speed of the sun. Above all, they calculated with astonishing accuracy the duration of the various lunar months, and, if they did not fully grasp the data of the problem of solar eclipses, they determined the conditions under which those of the moon took place. Finally, —and this was a still more arduous and complicated problem, —having determined the periods of the sidereal and synodic revolutions of the planets, they constructed perpetual ephemerides giving year by year the variations in the position of these five stars; then in the second century before our era they became so bold as to attempt an *a priori* calculation of planetary phenomena, such as they had previously worked out for the moon and the sun.

We have been obliged to introduce into this description certain technical details in order to fix exactly the period at which Chaldean science became established. It was not, as we have been asked to believe, in the remote obscurity of the fourth or even the fifth millennium that the mighty fabric of their astronomy was reared. It was during the first millennium that it was laboriously and gradually constructed. From this it follows that in Babylonia and in Greece, the two nations among whom the methodical study of the heavens led to the construction of systems which imposed themselves on the world, the development of these theories was partly contemporaneous. In the sixth century, when Thales is said to have predicted an eclipse, the Greeks began by being disciples of the Orientals, from whom they borrowed the rudiments of their knowledge.

But towards the middle of the fifth century they soared aloft on their own wings and soon reached greater heights than their former teachers.

The Babylonians after all had studied astronomy only empirically. By applying to it trigonometry, of which their predecessors were ignorant, the Greeks attained a certainty hitherto unknown, and obtained results previously impossible. But for several centuries the development of the two sciences went on side by side in East and West, and to a large extent independently. It would now be impossible to say to whom amongst the Greeks or the Babylonians belongs the credit of certain discoveries.[1] But it is the peculiar distinction of the Chaldeans that they made *religion* profit by these new conceptions and based upon them a learned theology. In Greece science always remained laic, in Chaldea it was sacerdotal.

❧   ❧

There is every reason for believing that religious origins were much the same among the Babylonians as among other Semitic peoples. Here as elsewhere differentiation comes only with progress. Numerous traces are found of a primitive "animism" which regarded as divinities animals, plants, and stones, as well as wind, rain, and storm, and believed them to have mysterious relations with mankind. Being experts in divination, the Chaldeans devoted themselves from the first to the practice of deriving omens from phenomena and occurrences in which they saw manifestations of the will of that motley host of spirits which filled the universe: movements of the clouds, direction of the wind, thunder and lightning, earthquakes and floods, as well as the birth of monstrous animals, the inspection of the liver, or even the appearance of locusts seemed to be portents favourable or unfavourable to human undertakings. All this was set down in writing and codified by the priests—for, every kind of superstition was codified by these Semites as well as the laws of Hammurabi. But among the countless multitude of gods who peopled the realm of nature, the Babylonians attributed a particularly

[1] See below, Lecture II, p. 26, on the cycle of Meton.

powerful influence to the stars. These brilliant objects, which they saw moving unceasingly over the vault of heaven,—conceived as a solid dome quite close to the earth,—inspired them with superstitious fear. Any one who has experienced the impression produced by the splendour of an Eastern night will understand this sense of awe. They believed that in the complicated patterns of the stars, which gleamed in the night, they could recognise fantastic shapes of polymorphous monsters, of strange objects, of sacred animals, of imaginary personages,— some of which still figure on our celestial maps. These formidable powers might be favourable or inimical. In the clearness of their transparent atmosphere the Chaldean priests continually watched their puzzling courses: they saw them appear and disappear, hide themselves under the earth to return at the other extremity of the horizon, rising again to a new life after a transitory death, always victorious over the darkness; they observed them losing themselves in the brilliance of the sun to emerge from it presently, like a young bridegroom entering the bridal chamber to issue forth again in the morning; they followed also the windings of the planets, whose complicated path seemed to aim at throwing off the track an enemy who threatened their course; they were astonished that in eclipses the moon and even the sun himself could grow dim, and they believed that a huge black dragon devoured them or concealed them from view. The sky was thus unceasingly the scene of combats, alliances, and amours, and this marvellous spectacle gave birth to a luxuriant mythology in which there appeared, subject to no law but their own passions, all the heroes of fable, all the animals of creation, all the phantoms of imagination.

Between beings and objects, all alike conceived as living, primitive animism everywhere establishes hidden and unexpected relations, which it is the object of magic to discover and utilise. In particular, the influence which the stars exerted upon our world seemed undeniable. Did not the rising and setting of the sun every day bring heat and cold, as well as light and darkness? Did not the changes of the seasons correspond to a certain state of the sky? What wonder, therefore, that by induction men arrived at the conclusion that even the lesser stars and their conjunctions had a certain connection with the phenomena of nature and the events of human life. At an early time—and here the Pan-Babylonists are right—arose the idea that the configuration of the sky corresponds to the phenomena of the earth. Everything in sky and earth alike is incessantly changing, and it was thought that there existed a correspondence between the movements of the gods above and the alterations which occurred here below. This is the fundamental idea of astrology. Perhaps in this scheme of coincidences the Babylonians even went so far as to divide the firmament into countries, mountains, and rivers, corresponding to the geography known to them.

Here, as everywhere, the human mind long sought the way of truth in the maze of conjectures and chimeras. But the very delusion which peopled the heavenly abodes with kindly or hostile powers, whose incessant evolutions were a menace or a promise to mankind, urged the Chaldeans to study assiduously their appearances, evolutions, and disappearances. With indefatigable patience they observed them, and noted the most important social or political events which had accompanied or followed such and such an aspect of the heavens, in order to assure themselves that a given coincidence would be regularly repeated. Thus they engraved on their tablets with scrupulous care all the astronomical or meteorological phenomena from which they derived their prognostications: phases of the moon, situation and conjunctions of the planets, eclipses, comets, falls of aerolites, and halos.

The purely empirical and very simple determinations, accompanied by predictions, which have been preserved to us, are naïve and almost puerile: even in the time of the Sargonides there is nothing in them which recalls the learned precision of a Greek horoscope. But from this mass of documents, laboriously collected in the archives of the temples, the laws of the movements of the heavenly bodies were disengaged with increasing precision. Primitive man commonly believes that new stars are produced each time they disappear, that the sun dies and is born each day or at least each winter, that the moon is swal-

lowed up during eclipses, and that another takes its place. To
these early ideas, all vestiges of which did not disappear, nay,
have not disappeared—we speak still of a "new moon"—
there succeeded the discovery that the same stars always
traversed the upper spheres with a brightness which increased
and diminished by turns. With the irregularity of atmospheric
disturbances was necessarily contrasted the regularity of sidereal revolutions and occultations. Little by little the priestly
astronomers, as we have seen, succeeded in constructing an
astronomical calendar and foretelling the return, at a fixed
date, of phenomena previously described, and they were able
to predict to the astonished crowds the arrival of the eclipses
which terrified them. There is nothing surprising in the fact
that, as they ascribed to the heaven itself the revelation of this
marvellous knowledge, they should have seen in astronomy a
divine science.

It is impossible to exaggerate the religious importance which
an eminently superstitious people attached to these discoveries.
Schiaparelli, a most competent historian of the exact sciences
in antiquity, has remarked that "the tendency which dominates
the whole Babylonian astronomy is to discover all that is
periodic in celestial phenomena, and to reduce it to a numerical
expression in such a manner as to be able to *predict* its repetition
in the future." [1] The scientific discoveries which were made from
the Assyrian period onwards enabled astrologers, as we have
seen, to foresee certain events with an absolute certainty which
no other kind of prognostication attained. An endless per-
spective reaching far into the future was opened to minds
astonished at their own audacity. Divination by means of the
stars was thus elevated above all other methods which were in
contemporary use. It is beyond doubt that the pre-eminence
henceforth assigned to astrology was bound to lead to a transformation of the whole of theology. "The science of the
observation of the heavens, which had been perfected little by
little by the priests, became in their hands a body of astral
doctrine, which never lost the flavour of the school, but which

---

[1] Schiaparelli, *I Primordi ed i Progressi dell' Astronomia presso i Babilonesi* (Extr. of
"*Scientia*," *Rivista di Scienza*, iii), Bologna, 1908, p. 22.

nevertheless permeated the entire Babylonian religion, and at least in part transformed it." [1]

The development of the old Babylonian religion bears no relation to astronomical theories. It was rather political circumstances which gave to certain gods in turn the primacy among the multitude of divinities worshipped in the land of Sumer and Accad, and, in accordance with a process which is repeated everywhere, caused the functions of other local powers to be attributed to their all-usurping and all-absorbing personality. When Babylon is the capital of the kings, it is the patron of this city, Marduk, identified with Bel, that occupies the foremost place in the Pantheon; when Nineveh is the seat of empire, it is Ashur. Even the groupings and hierarchies, which most plainly betray the intervention of priestly combination, do not appear to be prompted by astronomical speculations. In the system of triads, which theologians conceived, the primacy was given to Anu, Enlil, and Ea, spirits of Heaven, Earth, and Water; below these they placed Sin, Shamash, or Ramman, and Ishtar, the genii of the Sun and the Moon or the atmosphere and the goddess of the fertility of the earth, identified with the planet Venus. In spite of the presence in this symmetrical arrangement of the two luminaries at all times worshipped in that country, and sometimes of the most brilliant of the stars, it is impossible to see an astral principle in this grouping. Prof. Jastrow, the best judge in these matters, does not hesitate to regard the truly sidereal cult, which grew up at Babylon under the influence of the learned theories developed by the priestly caste, as *a new religion*. I quote his words: [2]

The Star-worship which developed in Babylon and Assyria in connection with the science of the observation of the heavens was at bottom a new religion, the victory of which brought about the decadence of the old popular belief. In point of fact, in the ritual of worship, in ceremonies of incantation and purification, in hymns and prayers, in the chants of ceremonial lamentation, in old festivals in honour of the gods of nature, just as in hepatoscopy (or

[1] Jastrow, *Die Religion Babyloniens und Assyriens*, ii, p. 432.
[2] Jastrow, *op. cit.*, ii, p. 455.

examination of the livers of victims) and in the other kinds of divination, which were maintained up to the end of the Babylonian empire, popular ideas always survived. The priests would have been careful not to destroy or imperil the dominion which they exercised over the multitude by changing the forms of worship in the direction of the new religion. But astral doctrines could not, for all that, fail to make their influence felt little by little as a dissolvent force.

The new doctrines were reconciled or combined after a fashion with the old creeds by placing the abode of the gods in the stars, or by identifying them with the latter. By a logical and fully justified development of primitive belief, which attributed to the sun and moon a powerful effect upon the earth, a preponderating influence over the determination of destiny had also been assigned to the five planets, which like the former traversed the constellations of the zodiac. These were therefore identified with the principal figures of the Assyrio-Babylonian pantheon. In accordance with the rank which was assigned to them and in accordance also with the brightness, colour, or duration of the revolution of the stars, relations were established between stars and gods. To Marduk, the foremost of the latter, was assigned Jupiter, whose golden light burns most steadily in the sky, Venus fell to Ishtar, Saturn to Ninib, Mercury to Nebo, Mars, by reason of its blood-red colour, to Nergal, patron of war. As for the fixed stars, singly or grouped in constellations, they were correlated with the less important lords, heroes, or genii. This was no impediment to regarding Ishtar, for instance, always as the goddess of the fertility of the earth, and worshipping her as such. Thus, as in the paganism of the Roman period, divinities assumed a double character, the one traditional and based on ancient beliefs, the other adventitious and inspired by learned theories.

The origin of this religious evolution goes back far into the past, but we are not able at the present day to mark the stages of its development and to assign dates to them. Perhaps it will be possible some day to follow the progress of Babylonian astronomy in the cuneiform tablets, and to show how an ever-widening conception of the heavens little by little transformed the modes of belief. Doubtless the theories of astronomers never completely eliminated the naïve tales which tradition related about the divine stars; here, as elsewhere, the enquiry into physical causes failed to get rid of mythical survivals, and the doctrines of oriental cosmographers continued to be encumbered with absurd notions. In order to be convinced on this point it is sufficient to glance at the astronomic curiosities of the Book of Enoch, which as late as the first century before our era echoes the old Chaldean doctrines.

It may be regarded as proved that this astral religion succeeded in establishing itself in the sixth century B.C., during the period of the short-lived glory of the second Babylonian empire, and after its fall, when new ideas derived from East and West were introduced, first by the Persians and afterwards by the Greeks, into the valley of the Euphrates.[1] If, as we shall show,[2] the Platonic dialogue, the *Epinomis*, is inspired by this religion, it had already formulated some of its chief dogmas before the fourth century. The essential characteristics of its theology are known to us, not from native texts, but from the information supplied by Western writers on "Chaldean" beliefs. The word Χαλδαῖος, *Chaldaeus*, bore amongst the ancients very different meanings from time to time. These terms designated first of all the inhabitants of Chaldea, that is, lower Mesopotamia, and next the members of the Babylonian priesthood. Thus at the period of the Achæmenid kings, in the official processions of Babylon, there walked first the *magi*, as Quintus Curtius states,[3] that is to say the Persian priests established in the conquered capital, then the *Chaldaei*, that is the native sacerdotal body. Later the epithet Χαλδαῖος was applied as a title of honour to the Greeks who had studied in the Babylonian schools and proclaimed themselves disciples of the Babylonians; finally it served to denote all those charlatans who professed to foretell the future according to the stars. The variations in meaning of this ethnical term, which ultimately became, like the term *magi*, a professional designation, have produced in turn an immense exaggeration of the anti-

---

[1] Jastrow, *l. c.*
[2] See below, Lecture II, p. 28.
[3] Quint. Curtius, v, 1, 22.

quity, or an undue depreciation of the worth, of the data furnished us by Diodorus Siculus,[1] Philo of Alexandria, and other writers on the religious and cosmic system of the "Chaldeans." These pieces of information, as might be expected, are of value only for the period immediately preceding these authors. They apply to those conceptions which were current among the priests of Mesopotamia under the Seleucids at the moment when the Greeks entered into continuous relations with them. Some of these conceptions are certainly very much older, and go back to ancient sacerdotal traditions. Diodorus contrasts the unity of the doctrines of the hereditary caste of the Chaldeans with the divergent views of the Greek philosophers on the most essential principles; but it is possible that the speculative mind of the Greeks had contributed to the clear formulation of these ancient beliefs and to the co-ordination of the dogmas of this religion, as it had done also in the case of astrology, which is a part of that religion.

🙐   🙒

The following are the broad lines of this theology.

From the leading fact established by them, namely, the invariability of the sidereal revolutions, the Chaldeans had naturally been led to the idea of a Necessity, superior to the gods themselves, since it commanded their movements; and this Necessity, which ruled the gods, was bound, *a fortiori*, to hold sway over mankind. The conception of a fatality linked with the regular movements of the heavens originated at Babylon, but this universal determinism was not there carried to its ultimate logical consequences. A sovereign providence had, it is true, by an irrevocable decree regulated the harmony of the world. But certain disturbances in the heavens, irregular occurrences such as appearances of comets or showers of falling stars, sufficed to maintain the belief in the exceptional operation of a divine will interfering arbitrarily in the order of nature. Priests foretold the future according to the stars, but by purifications, sacrifices, and incantations they professed to

---

[1] Diodor. Sic., ii, 29–31; Philo, *De Migr. Abrah.*, 32; *Quis Rerum div. Heres sit*, 20 etc.

drive away evils, and to secure more certainly the promised blessings. This was a necessary concession to popular beliefs which the very maintenance of the cult demanded. But under normal conditions, as experience proved, the divine stars were subject to an inflexible law, which made it possible to calculate beforehand all that they would bring to pass.

In oriental civilisations, which are priestly civilisations, the intimate union of learning and belief everywhere characterises the development of religious thought. But nowhere does this alliance appear more extraordinary than at Babylon, where we see a practical polytheism of a rather gross character combined with the application of the exact sciences, and the gods of heaven subjected to the laws of mathematics. This strange association is to us almost incomprehensible, but it must be remembered that at Babylon a *number* was a very different thing from a *figure*. Just as in ancient times and, above all, in Egypt, the *name* had a magic power, and ceremonial words formed an irresistible incantation, so here the number possesses an active force, the number is a symbol, and its properties are sacred attributes. Astrology is only a branch of mathematics, which the heavens have revealed to mankind by their periodic movements.

From their main discovery, that of the invariability of astronomical laws, the Chaldeans had deduced another important conclusion, namely, the eternity of the world. The world was not born in the beginning, it will not be subject to destruction in the future; a divine providence has from the outset ordered it as it shall be for ever. The stars, in fact, perform their revolutions according to ever invariable cycles of years, which, as experience proves, succeed each other to infinity. Each of these cosmic cycles will be the exact reproduction of those which have preceded it, for when the stars resume the same position, they are bound to act in precisely the same manner as before. The life of the universe, then, was conceived as forming a series of vast periods, which the most probable estimate fixed at 432,000 years. As early as the beginning of the third century before our era, Berosus, a priest of Bel, expounded to the Greeks the theory of the eternal return of

things, which Nietzsche prided himself on having discovered.

In the same way as it regarded numbers as sacred, this
religion of astronomers defied Time, the course of which was
bound up with the revolutions of the heavens. At regular
intervals it brought back the moon, the sun, the stars to their
starting-point, and as it seemed to govern their movements, it
was naturally regarded as a divine power. It was the heavenly
bodies that by their regular movements taught man to divide
into successive sections the unbroken chain of moments. Each
of the periods marked in the unending flight of time shared
the divinity of the stars, particularly the Seasons. In their worship old festivals of nature were combined with ideas derived
from astrology.

Babylonian theology had never entirely broken with the
primitive veneration with which Semitic tribes regarded all the
mysterious forces surrounding man. In the time of Hammurabi
the supreme triad was composed, as we have said, of the gods
of Heaven, Earth, and Water. Sidereal theology had systematised this very ancient cult of the powers of nature by connecting
them with astronomical theories. A vast pantheism had in-
herited and codified the ideas of ancient animism. The eternal
world is wholly divine, either because it is itself God, or because
it is conceived as containing within it a divine soul which per-
vades all things. The great reproach which Philo the Jew casts
upon the Chaldeans is precisely this, that they worship the
creation instead of the Creator.

This world is worshipped in its entirety, and worship is paid
also to its various parts: first of all, to Heaven, not only in
virtue of a reminiscence of the old Babylonian religion, which
gave the foremost place in the Pantheon to Anu, but also because it is the abode of the higher powers. Among the stars the
most important were conceived to be the moon and the sun,—
for it is in this order that they were placed,—then the five
planets, which were, as we have seen, dedicated to, or identified
with, the principal divinities of mythology. To them was given
the name of *Interpreters*, because, being endowed with a particular movement, not possessed by the fixed stars, which are

subject to a motion of their own, they above all others make manifest to man the purposes of the gods. But worship was also bestowed on all the constellations of the firmament, as the revealers of the will of Heaven, and in particular on the twelve signs of the zodiac, and the thirty-six decans, which were called the *Counsellor Gods*; then, outside the zodiac, on twenty-four stars, twelve in the northern, and twelve in the southern hemisphere, which, being sometimes visible, sometimes invisible, became the *Judges* of the living and the dead. All these heavenly bodies, whose variable movements and activities had been observed from the remotest times, announced not only hurricanes, rains, and scorching heats, but the good or evil fortune of countries, nations, kings, and even of mere individuals.

The domain of the divine god did not end at the zone of the moon, which is the nearest to us. The Chaldeans also worshipped, as beneficent or formidable powers, the Earth, whether fruitful or barren, the Ocean and the Waters that fertilise or devastate, the Winds which blow from the four points of the horizon, Fire which warms and devours. They confounded with the stars under the generic name of Elements (στοιχεῖα) these primordial forces, which give rise to the phenomena of nature. The system which recognises only four elements, prime sources of all things, is a creation of the Greeks.

If all the movements of the heavens inevitably have their reactions upon the earth, it is, above all, the destiny of man that depends upon them. The Chaldeans admitted, it appears, that the principle of life, which warms and animates the human body, was of the same essence as the fires of heaven. From these the soul received its qualities at birth, and at that moment the stars determined its fate here below.[1] Intelligence was divine, and allowed the soul to enter into relations with the gods above. By contemplating the stars the faithful received from them the revelation of all knowledge as well as all prescience. The priestly astrologers were always to some extent visionaries, who regarded as inspirations from on high all the ideas which sprang up in their own minds. Doubtless they had already conceived the idea that after death pious souls re-

[1] See below, Lecture II, p. 31.

ascend to the divine stars, whence they came, and in this celestial abode obtain a glorious immortality.[1]

To sum up, at the moment when the Greeks conquered Mesopotamia under Alexander, they found above a deep substratum of mythology a learned theology, founded on patient astronomical observations, which professed to reveal the nature of the world regarded as divine, the secrets of the future, and the destinies of man. In our next lecture we shall attempt to show what influence the Babylonian religion in contact with Hellenism exerted and underwent in turn, and how it was combined with the Stoic philosophy.

[1] See below, Lecture VI.

LECTURE II. *Babylon and Greece*

The relations of Greek philosophy with oriental theologies form a subject of vast extent, which has long been discussed. In this lecture we do not pretend to solve these problems or even to cover the whole ground which they embrace. Our interest is confined to one particular point, namely, when and how Semitic star-worship came to modify the ancient beliefs of the Hellenes.

Every sidereal cult, properly so called, was originally foreign to the Greeks as to the Romans—a fact which undoubtedly proves that the common ancestors of the Italians and the Hellenes dwelt in a northern land, where the stars were frequently concealed by fogs or obscured by clouds. For them nearly all the constellations remained a nameless and chaotic mass, and the planets were not distinguished from the other stars. Even the sun and the moon, although they were regarded as divinities, like all the powers of nature, occupied but a very secondary place in the Greek religion. Selene does not appear to have obtained anywhere an organised cult, and in the few places where Helios had temples, as for instance in the island of Rhodes, a foreign origin may reasonably be suspected.

Aristophanes characterises the difference between the religion of the Greeks and that of the barbarians by observing that the latter sacrifice to the Sun and the Moon, the former to personal divinities like Hermes. The pre-Hellenic populations very probably shared the worship of "the barbarians" of whom Aristophanes speaks, and survivals are found in popular customs and beliefs. Perhaps, also, certain distant reminiscences of the original naturalism of the Aryan tribes led the common people to regard the stars as living beings. It was a shock to popular belief when Anaxagoras maintained that they were merely bodies in a state of incandescence. But although the piety of the multitude was full of reverence for the great celestial luminaries, rulers of the day and of the night, the cities did not build temples to them. The cult of these cosmic powers had been eliminated by anthropomorphism.

From the days of Homer the gods are no longer physical agents, but moral—or, if you like, immoral—beings. Resembling men in their passions, they are their superiors in power alone; the close resemblance of their feelings to those of their devotees leads them to mingle intimately in the earthly life of the latter; inspired by a like patriotism they take part with the opposing hosts in the strifes of the cities, of which they are the official protectors; they are the protagonists in all the causes which are espoused by their worshippers. These immortal beings, whose image has been impressed upon the world by an aristocratic epic, are but faintly distinguished from the warrior heroes who worship them, save by the radiance of eternal youth. And sculptors, by investing them with a sovereign grace and a serene majesty, enabled them to elevate and ravish the souls of men by the mere sight of their imperishable beauty. The whole spirit of the Hellenic religion, profoundly human, ideally æsthetic, as poets and artists had fashioned it, was opposed to the deification of celestial bodies, far-off powers, devoid of feeling and of plastic form.

But though the prevalent worship and the city cults turned from the stars to venerate the august company of Olympians, though Apollo in the guise of a radiant youth eclipses the material brilliance of Helios, yet we find that the *philosophers* assign a place of honour to these same luminaries in their pantheon. Their systems, from the days of the Ionian physicists, revive and justify the old naturalistic beliefs, which were never entirely eradicated from the popular creed. Already in the eyes of Pythagoras the heavenly bodies are divine, moved by the ethereal soul which informs the universe and is akin to man's own soul. Plato accuses Anaxagoras of favouring atheism by his daring assertion that the sun is merely an incandescent mass and the moon an earth. Below the supreme eternal Being, who unites in himself every perfection, Plato would have us recognise the stars as "visible gods," which He animates with his own life, and which manifest his power. To the reformer's mind these celestial gods are infinitely superior to those of the popular religion. This conception of the great idealist, to whom the theology of the ancient and even that of the modern world owes more than to any other thinker, was to be developed by his successors, and in their hands astronomy became almost a sacred science. With no less pious zeal, Plato's rival, Aristotle, defends the dogma of the divinity of the stars: in them, as in the First Cause itself, he sees eternal substances, principles of movement, and therefore divine; and this doctrine, which thus forms an integral part of his metaphysic, was to disseminate itself throughout the ages and throughout the world, wherever the authority of the Master was recognised.

In deifying the celestial bodies, these philosophers may have been influenced by the desire of recommending to the veneration of their disciples beings more pure than those whom mythology represented as the sorry heroes of ridiculous or indecent legends, and to whom fable attributed all sorts of mischievous and shameful deeds. The polemics of the early rationalists had discredited these absurd or odious myths, and the deification of the stars, while saving polytheism, which was practically indestructible, suppressed anthropomorphism, which Xenophanes had already attacked so resolutely. The new sidereal theology has all the appearance of a compromise between popular beliefs and pure monotheism.

The philosophers may also have been led to this view, I readily grant, by the logical development of their own thought: the unceasing movement of these enormous masses showed that they were living beings, and the eternal immutability of their orbits proved that a superior reason directed their everlasting course. The admirable harmony of their relations, the inevitable, as well as the perennial, regularity of their revolutions implied the presence of a divine essence in them.

All this is quite true: practical motives and theoretical reasons may have simultaneously influenced these thinkers. But nevertheless it is impossible to doubt that in their attempts at the reformation of religion they were also inspired by the example which was set by the nations of the Orient. The

Greeks, who owed the fundamental axioms of their uranography to the Babylonians, would not fail to be struck also by
the lofty character of a star-worship which had become
scientific. The elements of their sidereal theology were, in all
probability, derived from external sources together with the
rudiments of their astronomy.

Here we touch a question which is very extensive and still
very obscure, in spite of the interminable discussions which it
has provoked,—or perhaps by reason of these impassioned
discussions. The history of the intellectual development of the
ancient world offers perhaps no more fundamental problem
than that of the influence which Babylonian science exercised
on Greece.

Recently, as we have observed, a certain school of Assyrio-
logists has curiously exaggerated the extent of this influence,
and the excesses of the "Pan-Babylonists" have provoked a
well-founded distrust of those fanciful views which see in
Chaldea the mother of all wisdom. But the reality of Hellenic
borrowings from Semitic sources remains none the less indisputable. At a distant date Hellas received from the far East
a duodecimal or sexagesimal system of measurement, both of
time and of objects. The habit of reckoning in terms of twelve
hours which we still use to-day, is due to the fact that the
Ionians borrowed from the Orientals this method of dividing
the day. Besides the acquaintance with early instruments, such
as the sun-dial,[1] they owed to the observatories of Mesopotamia
the fundamental data of their celestial topography: the ecliptic,
the signs of the zodiac, and the majority of the planets. To this
first influx of positive knowledge corresponds a first introduction into the Greek systems of the mystic ideas which Orientals
attached to them. I will not lay stress on the doubtful traditions
which make Pythagoras a disciple of the Chaldeans, but it has
proved possible to demonstrate that his system of numbers and
geometrical figures, designed to represent certain gods, is in
accordance with astrological theories. The dodecagon bears
the name of Jupiter because this planet traverses the circle of

---

[1] Γνώμων, Herod., ii, 109.

the zodiac in twelve years, that is to say, each year it traverses an arc terminated by the angles of the polygon which is inscribed in that circle.

But these first scientific and religious importations are assigned to a period when, as we know, the commercial cities of Ionia threw open their gates to Asiatic influences. It is more important to collect the traces of these Chaldean infiltrations after the Persian wars when Greek thought had achieved its autonomy. Certain facts recently brought to light indicate that the relations, direct or indirect, between the centres of Babylonian learning and of Greek culture, were never at any time entirely broken off.[1]

It is known that Meton passes as the inventor of a cycle of nineteen years (*enneakaidekaëteris*) which would establish a periodic agreement between the old lunar year and the solar revolutions, and which replaced the ancient *octaëteris*, or cycle of eight years, up to that time in use. The Golden Number[2] of our calendars still reminds us how, according to the tradition, this discovery, communicated to the Athenians in the year 432, excited their admiration to such a degree that they caused the calculations of Meton to be engraved in golden characters in the Agora. All this is, however, a fable. Since an *octaëteris* is proved to have been in use at Babylonia, by documents of the sixth century, and an *enneakaidekaëteris* by inscriptions of the fourth century, and this latter may well be much older, it seems difficult to believe that Meton was not prompted by the example which the Orientals set him. This is the more probable because he would appear to have had some superficial acquaintance with astrology, if we may believe that, at the moment of the departure of the fleet for Sicily, his science revealed to

[1] Kugler, *Im Bannkreis Babels*, 1910, p. 116 ss. See for other proofs my paper, *Babylon und die Griechische Astrologie* (Neue Jahrb. f. das klass. Altertum, xxvii), (1911), 1 ss.

[2] The "Golden Number" of the ecclesiastical calendar indicates the number of any year in the cycle of nineteen years which brings round the phases of the moon at the same dates. The dates of these phases in any year are thus the same as in other years which have the same "Golden Number."

him the disaster which awaited that expedition. It is true that it is always possible to maintain that the Babylonians and the Greeks arrived independently at the same conclusions, or even to go so far as to assert that the former were the imitators of the latter.

But here is a more convincing argument. When the Greeks learned to recognise the five planets known in antiquity, they gave them names derived from their character. Venus, whose brightness Homer had already celebrated, was called "Herald of the Dawn" ('Εωσφόρος) or "Herald of Light" (Φωσφόρος) or on the other hand "Vespertine" ("Εσπερος), according as she was considered as the star of the morning or that of the evening (the identity of these two being not yet recognised). Mercury was named the "Twinkling Star" (Στίλβων), Mars, because of his red colour, the "Fiery Star" (Πυρόεις), Jupiter the "Luminous Star" (Φαέθων), Saturn the "Brilliant Star" (Φαίνων), or perhaps, taking the word in another sense, the "Indicator." Now, after the fourth century other titles are found to supersede these ancient names, which are gradually ousted from use. The planets become the stars of Hermes, Aphrodite, Ares, Zeus, Kronos, ('Ερμοῦ, 'Αφροδίτης κτλ. ἀστήρ). Now this seems due to the fact that in Babylonia these same planets were dedicated respectively to Nebo, Ishtar, Nergal, Marduk, and Ninib. In accordance with the usual procedure of the ancients, the Greeks substituted for these barbarous divinities those of their own deities who bore some resemblance to them. Clearly exotic ideas, the ideas of Semitic star-worship, have come in here, for the ancient mythology of Hellas did not put the stars under the patronage of the Olympians nor establish any connection between them. Thus the names of the planets which we employ to-day, are an English translation of a Latin translation of a Greek translation of a Babylonian nomenclature.

Perhaps some doubt might still remain, if we did not see at the same time some very peculiar beliefs of the sidereal religion of Babylon creeping into the doctrines of the philosophers. It is a well-known fact that this religion formed a triad, Sin, Shamash, and Ishtar. To the god of the Moon, regarded as

the most powerful of the three, and to the Sun had been added
Venus, the most brilliant of the planets. These are the three
great rulers of the zodiac, and their symbols,—crescents, discs,
containing a star of four or six points—appear on the top of the
boundary pillars (*kudurru*) from the fourteenth century B.C.
Now the same association is found in an extract from Demo-
critus, where the Sun, the Moon, and Venus are distinguished
from the other planets.[1] The echo of the same theory extended
even to the Romans. Pliny, in a passage which owes its erudition to some Chaldean author of the Hellenistic period,[2]
remarks that Venus is "the rival of the Sun and the Moon,"
and he adds that "alone among the stars she shines with
such brilliance that her rays cast a shadow,"—a statement
which would be absurd in the climate of Rome, but which is
strictly correct under the clear sky of Syria.

Another instance of borrowing is still more obvious. To
Babylonian astrologers Saturn is the "planet of the Sun," he is
the "Sun of the night,"[3] that is to say, according to a system
of substitutions, of which there are many examples, Saturn
could take in astrological combinations the place of the star of
day when the latter had disappeared. Diodorus was well aware
of this fact. When explaining (11, 30) that the Chaldeans
designate the planets as "the Interpreters" (ἑρμηνεῖς), because by their course they reveal to men the will of
the gods, he adds: "the star which the Greeks name Kronos
they call the 'star of the Sun,' because it is the most
prominent, and gives the most numerous and most important
predictions."

Now in the *Epinomis* of Plato,—it matters little in this
connection whether this be a work of the Master himself in his
old age, or whether it was composed by his pupil, Philip of
Opus, who after copying the Laws may have added this
appendix,—there is an allusion to this peculiar doctrine. In
the enumeration of the planets which is there made it is stated
that the slowest of them all bears according to some people

[1] Diels, *Doxographi Graeci*, p. 344, 16=*Fragm. der Vorsokratiker*, p. 366, 22.
[2] Plin., *Nat. Hist.*, ii, 36.
[3] Jastrow, *Revue d'Assyriologie*, vii, 1910, ss.p. 163

the name of Helios.[1] Moreover, the fact that the writer was acquainted with oriental theories comes out no less clearly from certain expressions of which he makes use in this passage, than from the very object which he has in view. He dreamed of a reconciliation between the cult of Apollo of Delphi, and that of the sidereal gods which the piety of Syria and Egypt had taught to the Greeks. According to him it behoved the Greeks to perfect this worship of the stars, recently introduced into their country, as they had perfected everything which they had received from the barbarians. These phrases, in which Hellenic pride is clearly revealed, while at the same time there slips in a confession of dependence on the foreigner, are highly characteristic. Their whole significance is apparent now that a typical detail has revealed to us what the author's astronomical learning owes to the Chaldeans. Hereafter perhaps it will be proper to attach some importance to a note preserved in a papyrus of Herculaneum,[2] and due, it seems, to this very Philip of Opus to whom the composition of the *Epinomis* is attributed. It would appear that Plato in his old age received a "Chaldean" guest, who was able to instruct him in the discoveries made by his compatriots.

It seems to me to be beyond doubt that the influence of oriental star-worship upon the *Epinomis* was much more extensive than has hitherto been admitted. It is not from the Pythagoreans that the author borrows, but, as he himself says, from the Syrians. We find set forth or indicated in this brief dialogue the fundamental doctrines, of which we have already seen some expressly attributed to the Chaldeans, while others we shall find developed in the stellar theology of the Roman period.

These doctrines are the idea that science in general is a gift of the gods, and that mathematics in particular were revealed to men by Uranus, considered as a deity, who caused them to be understood by his periodical phenomena; the demonstration

[1] As a matter of fact, certain copyists, not understanding the meaning of this identification, have inserted as a correction "of Kronos," but the reading of the best manuscripts is ʿΗλίου not Κρόνου, as has been observed by Bidez, *Rev. de Philol.*, xxix (1905), p. 319.

[2] *Academicorum Phil. Ind. Hercul.*, ed. Mekler, p. 13, col. iii, 36.

that, whatever may be the opinion of the vulgar, the stars are animated and divine, and that between these celestial divinities and the earth a hierarchically organised army of airy spirits acts as intermediary; the declaration that the most perfect of the sciences is astronomy, which has become a theology. Man, the author says, attracted by the beauty of the visible world, does not merely conceive the desire of knowing all that his nature allows him to apprehend, he rises to a fervent contemplation of the wondrous spectacle of harmonious movements, which surpass all choruses in majesty and magnificence. This study, in short, is inseparable from virtue; this wisdom secures supreme happiness, and it has as its reward in the next world a life of bliss like that which the pious astronomer has led on earth, but more perfect, a life in which he will be entirely absorbed in the contemplation of celestial splendours, and will attain to supreme felicity.

Truly the *Epinomis* is that which it professes to be: the first gospel preached to Hellenes of the stellar religion of Asia. The ideas which are here set forth will not cease to influence the Platonic school. Thus Xenocrates, to whom astronomy is a sacred science, will develop demonology, and we shall see how an eclectic, Posidonius, will expand and exalt these same conceptions.

❧   ❧

But, it will be said, if the Greeks thus bowed to the supremacy of the sidereal theology of the Chaldeans, how was it that astrology was not introduced among them? For from the sixth to the fourth century the whole marvellous development of their philosophy shows that it knows nothing of cosmic fatalism and stellar divination. Speaking generally, this assertion is correct, although certain traces of these speculations are found, as we have seen, in works of the early Pythagoreans, and recently a Chaldean doctrine has been successfully employed to explain a passage of Pindar.[1] Now, about the period when Philip of Opus published or wrote the *Epinomis*, another pupil

[1] Franz Boll, *Neue Jahrb. für das klass. Altertum*, xxi (1908), p. 119.

of Plato, the astronomer Eudoxus of Cnidos, declared: "No
credence should be given to the Chaldeans, who predict and
mark out the life of every man according to the day of his
nativity."[1] Certain modern philologists—who doubtless look
upon Greek history as a kind of experiment in a closed vessel,
which a providence anxious to exclude every disturbing element conducted for the fullest instruction of the *savants* of the
future—certain philologists, I say, have doubted whether
Eudoxus in the fourth century could really have known and
condemned oriental genethlialogy. But like Eudoxus, Theophrastus, a little later, spoke of it in his treatise on "Celestial
Signs": he regarded with surprise the claim of the Chaldeans
to be able to predict from these signs the life and death of
individuals, and not merely general phenomena, such as good
or bad weather.[2]

The insatiable curiosity of the Greeks, then, did not ignore
astrology, but their sober genius rejected its hazardous doctrines, and their keen critical sense was able to distinguish the
scientific data observed by the Babylonians from the erroneous
conclusions which they derived from them. It is to their everlasting honour that, amid the tangle of precise observations and
superstitious fancies which made up the priestly lore of the
East, they discovered and utilised the serious elements, while
neglecting the rubbish.

As long as Greece remained Greece, stellar divination gained
no hold on the Greek mind, and all attempts to substitute an
astronomic theology for their immoral but charming idolatry
were destined to certain failure. The efforts of philosophers to
impose on their countrymen the worship of "the great visible
gods," as Plato terms them, recoiled before the might of a
tradition supported by the prestige of art and literature. It was
a purely intellectual movement which remained, as it would
seem, without serious practical result. It changed neither
popular nor official worship. The populace continued to pray
"κατὰ τὰ πάτρια," after the fashion of their ancestors, to old

[1] Cic., *De Div.*, ii, 42, 87.
[2] Procl., *In Tim.*, iii, 151, 1 (Diehl). On Theophrastus' translation of the tale of
Akichar, see below, p. 38.

protectors of family and city, and the formulary of the old-fashioned liturgies remained unchanged in spite of all the objections which the science of the reformers could raise against it.

But after the conquests of Alexander a great change took place. The ancient ideal of the Greek republic gave way to the conception of universal monarchy. Thenceforth municipal cults disappeared before an international religion. The worship of the stars, common to all the peoples, was strengthened by everything that weakened the particularism of cities. In proportion as the idea of "humanity" spread, men were the more ready to reserve their homage for those celestial powers which extended their blessings to all mankind, and princes who proclaimed themselves the rulers of the world, could not be protected save by cosmopolitan gods.

Thus it was that thinkers agreed more and more in reserving the foremost place for the sidereal deities. Zeno and his disciples proclaimed their might still more clearly than the schools of Plato and Aristotle. Since stoic pantheism represented Reason, which governs all things, as residing in ethereal Fire, the stars in which the supreme Fire manifested itself with the greatest force and brilliance, would necessarily be invested with the loftiest divine qualities. In the same way the prodigious success attained by the doctrine of Euhemerus contributed to the exaltation of their power. This doctrine, we know, regarded the divinities of fable as superior mortals, to whom after death the gratitude or admiration of the multitude had accorded worship. In thus attributing to the Olympians of old no longer merely human form but also human nature, it left to the eternal and incorruptible stars alone the dignity of original gods, and exalted them in proportion as it lowered their rivals of bygone days.

Thus the political condition of the world, just as the tendencies of theology, drew Hellenism towards star-worship. But the interpenetration of the Orient and Greece which took place in this period, hastened this religious evolution in a remarkable manner. The Stoa, as we shall see, was freely accessible to barbaric influences, and Euhemerus, we are told, drew his inspiration from Egyptian theologoumena. But the decisive agency was the contact which was established in the Seleucid Empire between Hellenic culture and Babylonian civilisation.

The Chaldeans, whom the policy of the kings of Antioch strove to conciliate, entered into close relations with the learned men who came to Asia in the train of their conquerors, and they even proceeded to carry their precepts throughout the land of Greece. A priest of Bel, Berosus, established himself about the year 280 in the island of Cos, and there revealed to his sceptical hearers the contents of the cuneiform writings accumulated in the archives of his country, annals of the ancient kings and astrological treatises. Another Chaldean, Soudines, invited to the court of Attalus I, king of Pergamus, practised there, about the year 238, the methods of divination in vogue in his native land, such as inspection of the liver ($\dot{\eta}\pi\alpha\tau\sigma\sigma\kappa\sigma\pi\acute{\iota}\alpha$), and he continued to be an authority frequently quoted by the later "mathematici." On the other hand, Greek *savants* of repute, Epigenes of Byzantium, Apollonius of Myndus, Artemidorus of Parium, declared themselves the disciples of these same Chaldeans, and boasted of being instructed in their priestly schools. At the same time centres of Greek science were established in the heart of Mesopotamia, and in the ancient observatories of Bel learners were initiated into the methods and discoveries of the astronomers of Alexandria or Athens. Under the Seleucids and the early Arsacids Babylon was a hellenised city, as is proved by the epigraphical discoveries which have been made there. Of this interpenetration of oriental and occidental learning we can to-day quote some striking proofs. So it has quite recently been shown that a series of prognostications derived from earthquakes, thunderstrokes, or the course of the moon were literally translated from Assyrian texts into the Greek *Brontologia* and *Selenodromia*.[1] But though the reality of the relation between the two sciences and pseudo-

---

[1] Bezold and Boll, *Reflexe astrol. Keilinschriften bei Griechischen Schriftstellern* (Abhandl. Akad. Heidelberg), 1911.

sciences is uncontested and incontestable, there remains the difficulty of deciding in each case which of the two influenced the other.

Thus it has been maintained that the ancient Babylonians were already acquainted with the precession of the equinoxes,[1] but an examination of cuneiform tablets reveals the very important fact that they were ignorant of it at least up to about the end of the second century B.C. The credit of this discovery clearly belongs, therefore, to Hipparchus of Nicæa (about 161–126) as tradition asserts, and it is to him that the observatories of Mesopotamia owed the knowledge of it. But conversely, thanks to the recent publication of astrological treatises, it is possible to show that certain discoveries hitherto attributed to Hipparchus owe their origin in reality to some genuine Chaldeans. In one exceptional case we can detect a borrowing in the very act and indicate the intermediary who effected the transfer. Perhaps, then, some details will not be deemed superfluous here.[2]

The part of astronomy in which Babylonians pushed their investigators furthest was probably the determination of the course of the moon, which enabled them to predict the periodic return of eclipses. Undoubtedly this was one of the most ancient studies to which the people of that country directed their energies. Sin, the Moon-god, was in their eyes a more considerable divinity than the Sun, Shamash, himself. Before the duration of the year was known, the phases of the moon served to measure time, and to fix the dates of sacred calendars; moreover, the star of night allowed herself to be observed by the naked eye better than any other, and it was possible to follow almost continuously her winding course in the heavens. The experience, extending over thousands of years, of this priesthood of astrologers, had led them little by little to construct tables,

[1] See above, Lecture I, p. 3.
[2] See my paper *Babylon und die Griech. Astron.*, p. 6 ss., where the texts are fully given.

which had attained a high degree of precision at the moment when, under Alexander, the Greeks entered into direct relations with them. The remains of these tables have been deciphered and interpreted by F. X. Kugler, and, astonishing to relate, they have revealed to him a mistake which was introduced into, and, perpetuated in, the calculations of modern astronomers. The old notations of the Chaldeans have allowed a correction of the canons of Oppolzer! About the year 200 before our era these learned priests had succeeded in determining in advance not only the dates of the phases and eclipses of the moon, but also the principal phenomena of the five planets.[1] Although in general inclined to depreciate the value of Babylonian science, in opposition to those who have unduly exaggerated it, this most authoritative modern interpreter of it marvels at the aspect of these great tables with their numerous columns regularly arranged, of which the figures dovetail into each other like the cogwheels of a machine, and the arrangement of which is expounded in explanatory notes. "One does not know," he cries, "which to admire the more: the extraordinary accuracy of the periods which is implied by the drawing up of each of the columns of figures, or the ingenuity with which these old masters contrived to combine all the factors to be considered." Even before the cuneiform inscriptions had been deciphered, historians admitted that the Chaldeans had deduced from their empirical observations, amassed from generation to generation, a theory of the motions of the moon which influenced the development of Greek doctrines. Further, an evident proof of this is supplied by the fact that in the *Almagest* Ptolemy[2] quotes, after Hipparchus, the eclipses of the years 621, 523, 502, 491, 383 B.C., observed at Babylon, and the first of these has been found noted in an Assyrian text. How absolutely the astronomer of Nicæa relied on his oriental predecessors can be ascertained to-day from some figures. Ptolemy attributed to Hipparchus an extremely exact calculation of the lunar periods; but it has been possible to demonstrate that the duration which he assigns to the various

[1] See above, Lecture I, p. 9.
[2] Ptol., *Syntax.*, v, 14; iv, 8, 11.

months is precisely that which is laid down in the cuneiform tablets, namely:

Mean synodic   month 29 days 12 hours 44′ 31.3″
  „   sidereal   „   27 „   7   „   43′ 14 ″
  „   anomalistic   „   27 „ 13   „   18′ 34.9″
  „   dracontic   „   27 „   5   „   5′ 35.8″[1]

Clearly the priority of discovery belongs to the Orientals, as well as that of the inequality of the length of the seasons, of which they were perfectly aware.

But how did these data and these doctrines pass from the banks of the Euphrates to the Greek cities? Who was the intermediary between Hipparchus and the priests of Babylon? Documents recently published have revealed his name. Strabo, speaking of the schools of astronomers called "Chaldean," which existed in various towns of Mesopotamia, adds:[2] "Mathematicians frequently mention several of them, as Kidenas, Nabourianos, and Soudines." According to Pliny[3] the same Kidenas had recognised that Mercury is never more than 23° from the sun. This Kidenas was probably contemporary with Soudines, who lived in the second half of the third century before Christ.

Now the astrologer, Vettius Valens,[4] who wrote under the Antonines, tells us that he attempted to make for himself a canon of the sun and the moon for the purpose of determining eclipses, but, as time failed him, "he resolved to make use of Hipparchus for the sun, and Soudines, Kidenas and Apollonius for the moon . . . putting in their proper places the equinoxes and solstices at the eighth degree of the signs of the zodiac." Further, a passage in an anonymous commentary on Ptolemy[5] represents Kidenas as the inventor of an ecliptic period of 251

---

[1] The durations calculated by modern astronomers are:

  (1) 29 days 12 hours 44′ 2.9″
  (2) 27 „   7   „   43′ 11.5″
  (3) 27 „ 13   „   18′ 39.3″
  (4) 27 „   5   „   5′ 36″

[2] Strab., xvi, 1, 6, p. 639 C.
[3] Plin., *Nat. Hist.*, ii, 39.
[4] Vett. Val., *Anthol.*, ix, 11, p. 353, 22, ed. Kroll.
[5] Published, *Cat. Codd. Astr.* VIII, part ii, p. 125.

lunations (synodic months) and 269 anomalistic revolutions, the authorship of which was usually attributed to Hipparchus. It appears from this treatise that Hipparchus did not adopt simultaneously, as was believed, two ecliptic periods, one large, of 4267 lunations and 4573 anomalistic revolutions, and one small, one seventeenth of the former, consisting of 251 lunations and 269 anomalistic revolutions, but that he borrowed this latter from Kidenas and appears merely to have multiplied it by 17 in order to make it correspond to a nearly exact number of years, say 4612 sidereal revolutions (345 years) *minus* $7\frac{1}{2}°$.

Now on a lunar table engraved in the second century in cuneiform characters on 18 columns, a masterpiece of accuracy, can be read the signature *Ki-din-nu*, and though ordinary scribes add their father's name, *Ki-din-nu* is without any addition: he is the astronomer whom every one knew.

Schiaparelli had already suspected the identity of this personage with the Kidenas of the Greeks. Kugler has definitely proved it,[1] for the equivalence of 251 synodic and 269 anomalistic months, which Ptolemy's commentator attributes to him, is found precisely stated in this table of Kidinnu, and further the same table places the equinoxes and the solstices at the 8th degree of the signs of the zodiac, as did Valens, who quotes the canons of Kidenas. To Hipparchus, on the contrary, the commencement of spring is the 0° of the Ram, but the Roman calendars usually adopted the 8th degree in conformity with the ancient usage of Babylon.

Kidenas or Kidinnu, then, belongs to that group of hellenised Chaldeans of whom Berosus is the most illustrious representative, and who in the third century before our era devoted themselves to the task of rendering accessible to the Greeks the treasures of knowledge which were contained in the cuneiform documents amassed in the libraries of their native land. On these traditional data he based the hypothesis of a new ecliptic period more correct than that of his Chaldean predecessors, which was employed by Hipparchus and afterwards by Ptolemy. The very quotations which are made from his works by Western writers prove that he had them translated into

[1] Kugler, *Im Bannkreis Babels*, 1910, p. 122.

Greek and that he thus enriched Hellenic astronomy with these lunar canons, to which the observations taken at Babylon, extending over a long period of centuries, had given an admirable precision.

❧   ❧

Thus we see critical researches gradually determining the extent of the debt which Greece owes to Babylon, and substituting palpable realities for the huge and shadowy phantoms which wandered in the pre-historic twilight. The influence of the old oriental civilisation was not exercised solely on the domain of science, but also of literature. Prof. Diels of Berlin has recently pointed out [1] how the often satirical tales, in which trees and plants appear, belong to a class of fables popularised in Assyria before they were repeated by Callimachus in his *Iambics* and by the successors of Æsop. Further, the recent discovery of an Aramaic manuscript of the fifth century at Elephantine has enabled us to show how the romance of Akichar passed from the banks of the Euphrates to the Jewish communities of Palestine and Egypt (to which it furnished the motive of the book of Tobit) and reached Greece, where Theophrastus adopted it and immortalised the wise Akicharos. But above all, Babylon was to the men of old the mother of astronomy, as of star-worship. It is in this department more than all others that it is possible to show how the Greeks profited from the learned theories which had been formulated, and from the positive data which had been slowly accumulated by these ancient priests of Mesopotamia

Longa per assiduam complexi saecula curam. [2]

The constructive logic of the Greeks, combining with the patient labours of the indigenous race, produced in those days on the banks of the Euphrates an intellectual movement, too little known, which would perhaps have attained to the glory of Alexandrine science, if it had not been lamentably arrested in the latter half of the second century by the ravages of the

[1] Diels, *Orientalische Fabeln im Griechischen Gewande* (Internation. Wochenschrift f. Wiss., 6 Aug., 1910).
[2] Manil., i, 54.

Parthian invasion and the sack of Babylon. The Chaldeans themselves, emancipated from tradition, discussed freely the principles of the universe, and of the rival sects, which then sprang up at Borsippa, Orchoe, and elsewhere, some went so far as to reject as mendacious the very astrology which had been elaborated by their ancestors.[1] The most remarkable representative of this rationalistic movement is Seleucus of Seleucia, who may be either a Greek emigrant or a hellenised native. Giving up the firmament of primitive cosmogonies, he opened the infinite spaces of a limitless universe to the courses of the stars. Recurring to a bold hypothesis of Aristarchus of Samos, and advancing new arguments in its support, he showed that the sun is the centre of the world, and that the earth has a double motion, revolving round the sun and spinning on its own axis; at the same time he offered a better explanation than any one had previously propounded of the movement of the tides, which no doubt he had observed in the Persian Gulf, by referring them to the phases of the moon. Copernicus, who by the formulation of his heliocentric theory produced "the greatest revolution in the history of knowledge," seems to have been ignorant even of the name of his distant forerunner.

But the scientific rationalism of this Galileo of antiquity was destined to be condemned. It was opposed by the force of a thousand-year-old tradition, the anxious superstition of the mob, the haughty convictions and temporal interests of a powerful sacerdotal caste. The future belonged to a compromise, which, while respecting those ancient beliefs to which the majority of mankind was invincibly attached, would satisfy the demands of a more comprehensive intelligence. This conciliatory formula was discovered by stoicism. Everywhere it devoted itself to the task of justifying popular worships, sacred narratives, and ritual observances. In Greece, it was able without much difficulty to come to terms with cults more formalistic than doctrinal, more civic than moral, in which no authority demanded assent to definite dogmas. A system of accommodating allegories could readily put on gods or myths a physical, ethical, or psychological interpretation, which

[1] Strab., xvi, 1, 6.

reconciled them with the cosmology or ethics of the Porch. In the East, where more theological religions always implied a more definite conception of the world, the task appeared much less easy. Yet certain profound affinities reconciled stoicism with Chaldean doctrines. Whether these did or did not contribute to the development of the ideas of Zeno, they offer a singular analogy to his pantheism, which represented ethereal Fire as the primordial principle and regarded the stars as the purest manifestation of its power. Stoicism conceived the world as a great organism, the "sympathetic" forces of which acted and re-acted necessarily upon one another, and was bound in consequence to attribute a predominating influence to the celestial bodies, the greatest and the most powerful of all in nature, and its Εἱμαρμένη or Destiny, connected with the infinite succession of causes, readily agreed also with the determinism of the Chaldeans, founded, as it was, upon the regularity of the sidereal movements. Thus it was that this philosophy made remarkable conquests not only in Syria but as far as Mesopotamia. I recall only the fact that one of the masters of the Porch, the successor of Zeno of Tarsus at Athens, was Diogenes of Babylon (circa 240–150) and that, later on, another distinguished Stoic, Archidemus, founded a famous school at Babylon itself (second century B.C.). We know too little of their theories to determine what place was held in them by the beliefs of the country of their origin or of their adoption. We only perceive the result of this movement of ideas which was to lead to the entry of astrology and star-worship into the philosophy of Zeno. For us the person who almost alone represents this fusion of East and West is Posidonius of Apamea, of whom we shall speak in our next lecture,[1] but the preparations for this fusion were undoubtedly made by his predecessors. It is remarkable that the great astronomer, Hipparchus, whose scientific theories, as we have just seen, are directly influenced by Chaldean learning, was also a convinced supporter of one of the leading doctrines of stellar religion. "Hipparchus," says Pliny,[2] "will never receive all

---

[1] See below, Lecture III, p. 47.
[2] Plin., Nat. Hist., ii, 26, 95.

the praise he deserves, since no one has better established the relationship between man and the stars, or shown more clearly that our souls are particles of heavenly fire." In this passage we see affirmed as early as the second century before our era a conception, the development of which we follow in the sidereal mysticism of the Roman period.[1]

Hipparchus saw the ruin of the country where was born that science which he illumined. Invaded by the Parthians about the year 140 B.C., recaptured by Antiochus VII of Syria in 130, reconquered soon afterwards by King Phraates, Mesopotamia was terribly ravaged for more than a quarter of a century. Babylon, sacked and burned in 125, never recovered her former splendour: a progressive decay brought on her a death by slow consumption. The new Iranian princes evinced no solicitude for the culture of Semitic priests. The vast brick-built temples, when the hand of the restorer was withdrawn, crumbled into dust, one by one were extinguished the lights of a civilisation which extended backwards for forty centuries, and of the famous cities of Sumer and Accad there survived little but the name. The last astronomical tablet in cuneiform characters with which we are acquainted, is dated 8 B.C., and Strabo,[2] speaking of Babylon about the same period, applies to it a verse from a comic poet: "a mighty desert—such is the mighty town."

Henceforth it is far from their native land, in Syria, in Egypt, and in the West, that we must follow the development of the religious ideas derived from the Chaldea of antiquity.

[1] See below, Lecture V.
[2] Strab., xvi, 1, 5: Ἐρημία μεγάλη ᾿στιν ἡ Μεγάλη πόλις.

LECTURE III. *The Dissemination in the West*

We have seen the "Pan-Babylonist" mist, which obscured the historical horizon, vanish before the breath of criticism. It is not the fact that thousands of years before our era the Chaldeans constructed a learned and profound cosmology, which established its authority over all surrounding peoples. But their share in the intellectual and religious development of antiquity remains none the less most considerable. They are the creators of chronology and astronomy. They contrived to enlarge their theology progressively in order to keep it in harmony with their new conception of the world, and their astrology was regarded as the method of divination *par excellence*. Their conquests in the realm of science won such prestige for their beliefs that they spread from the Far East to the Far West, and even now their sway has not been wholly overthrown. In mysterious ways they penetrated as far as India, China, and Indo-China, where divination by means of the stars is still practised at the present day, and reached perhaps even the primitive centres of American civilisation. In the opposite direction they spread to Syria, to Egypt, and over the whole Roman world, where their influence was to prevail up to the fall of paganism and lasted through the Middle Ages up to the dawn of modern times. It is this dissemination throughout the West that we shall rapidly describe in this lecture.

☙   ❧

The exchange of religious ideas between the two rival empires of the valleys of the Euphrates and the Nile undoubtedly goes back, like their political relations, to a very remote antiquity. In the fifteenth century before our era, at the moment when—as the Tell-el-Amarna tablets show—Babylonian was the diplomatic language of the whole East, and

Egypt extended its empire or its suzerainty over the principali-
ties of Canaan and Syria, we find Amenophis IV ordaining the
exclusive worship of the Sun as lord of heaven and earth,
protector of his person and of his subjects of every nationality.
It is possible that this theological Pharaoh was led by the influence of Semitic star-worship to impose his attempt at reform
upon the Egyptian clergy. Many other proofs might be
advanced to show that the beliefs and even the cults of the
Syrians found their way into the state of the Pharaohs. But
the religious ideas with which we are particularly concerned
here were late in being introduced. Astrology was *unknown* in
ancient Egypt: it was not until the Persian period, about the
sixth century, that it began to be cultivated there. The ascendancy which it then acquired, succeeded in breaking down the
haughty reserve of the proudest and most exclusive people in
the world, and a conservative clergy was compelled to admit
to its ranks calculators of hours and makers of horoscopes
(ὡρολόγοι, ὡροσκόποι) devoted to the study of Chaldean
science. The history of this dissemination confirms what we
said both about the late date of this religious development in
Babylonia and about the irresistible prestige which the brilliant
discoveries of astronomy conferred upon it from the Assyrian
period onwards. This foreign religion was gradually naturalised
in Egypt: the huge zodiacs, which decorated the walls of the
temples, show how sacerdotal teaching succeeded in grafting
the learned doctrines of the Chaldeans on native beliefs and in
giving them an original development. National pride even
ended by convincing itself that all this religious erudition was
purely indigenous. About the year 150 B.C. there were composed in Greek—undoubtedly at Alexandria—the mystic
treatises attributed to the fabulous king Nechepso and his confidant, the priest Petosiris, which became as it were the sacred
books of the growing faith in the power of the stars. These
apocryphal works of a mythical antiquity were to acquire
incredible authority in the Roman world.

The god Tôt (Thoth), the Hermes Trismegistus of the Greeks,
became in Egypt the revealer of the wisdom of horoscopers, as
of all other kinds of wisdom. But it was a difficult task to

reconcile astrology with national beliefs, as Hermetism sought to do. For, astrology was not only a method of divination: it implied, as we have said, a religious conception of the world, and it was inseparably combined with Greek philosophy. Thus the Hermetic books comprise not merely treatises on learned superstition: it is a complete theology that the gods teach to the faithful in a series of what may be called apocalypses. This recondite literature, often contradictory, was apparently developed between 50 B.C. and A.D. 150. It has a considerable importance in relation to the diffusion throughout the Roman Empire of certain doctrines of sidereal religion moulded to suit Egyptian ideas. But it had only a secondary influence. It is not at Alexandria that this form of paganism was either produced or chiefly developed, but among the neighbouring Semitic peoples.

Syria, lying as it does nearer than Egypt to Babylon and Nineveh, was more vividly illumined by the radiance of those great centres of culture. The ascendancy of an erudite clergy who ruled there, was extended at an early date over all surrounding countries, eastwards over Persia, northwards over Cappadocia. But nowhere was it so readily accepted as among the Syrians, who were united with the Oriental Semites by community of language and blood.

The very names Σύριοι, "Syrian," and Ἀσσύριοι, "Assyrian," are originally identical, and for a long time the Greeks made no distinction between them. The plains of Mesopotamia and Cœle-Syria, inhabited by kindred races, extended across frontiers which are not marked out by nature, and, despite all political vicissitudes, relations between the great temples situated east and west of the Euphrates continued without interruption.

It is difficult to fix the date at which the influence of the "Chaldeans" began to be felt in Syria, but it is certainly not later than the period when the dominion of the Sargonides was extended as far as the Mediterranean, that is to say, the eighth century B.C.; and without admitting, with the Pan-Babylonists, that the stories of Genesis are merely astral myths, we may regard it as indisputable that before the Exile (597 B.C.) Israel

received from Babylon, along with some astronomical knowledge, certain beliefs connected with star-worship and astrology.
We know that idolatry was repeatedly introduced into Zion.
Thus king Manasseh caused the chariot of Shamash, the Sun-
god, to be accepted there; he dared to set the "Queen of the
Heavens" by the side of Iahweh. After the Exile, spiritual
relations were continuous between Judaism and the great
religious metropolis which had subjugated it. As late as the
first century B.C., the author of the Book of Enoch, in his
pretended revelations, is obviously inspired by Babylonian
cosmology and legends.

If Israel, which repulsed all forms of polytheism with such
inflexible determination, nevertheless yielded temporarily to
the prestige of star-worship, how much more effectively must
this cult have established its sway over Semitic tribes which had
remained pagan? Under its influence they are seen to adopt
new divinities: Bel of Babylon was worshipped all over northern
Syria. The ancient divinities also were grouped anew: At
Hierapolis, as at Heliopolis and Emesa, a new member was
added to the original pair, Baal and Baalat, husband and wife,
in order to form one of those triads of which Chaldean theology
was fond. But this theology profoundly modified, above all,
the conception of the higher powers reverenced by these
pastoral or agricultural tribes. Side by side with their proper
nature, it gave to these gods a second personality, which became none the less prominent because it was borrowed, and
sidereal myths came to be interlined, as it were, with agrarian
myths and soon obliterated them. From being lords of a clan
and a narrow district, the Baals were promoted to the dignity
of universal gods. The old spirit of storm and thunder, Baal
Shammin, who dwelt in the sky, becomes the Most High
($"Y\psi\iota\sigma\tau\sigma\varsigma$), the eternal regulator of cosmic movements.[1] The
naturalistic and primitive worship which these peoples paid to
the Sun, the Moon, and certain stars such as Venus, was
systematised by a doctrine which constituted the Sun—
identified with the Baals, conceived as supreme gods—the

[1] See my *Oriental Religions*, p. 127 ss.

almighty Lord of the world, thus paving the way in the East for the future transformation of Roman paganism.[1]

There can be no doubt that Babylonian doctrines exercised decisive influence on this gradual metamorphosis and this latest phase of Semitic religion. The Seleucid princes of Antioch showed as great deference to the science of the Babylonian clergy as the Persian Achæmenids had done before them. We find Seleucus Nicator consulting these official soothsayers about the propitious hour for founding Seleucia on the Tigris; and, if we may believe Diodorus,[2] these diviners made to Alexander, Antigonus, and numerous other monarchs predictions which were fulfilled to the letter. Antiochus, king of Commagene, who died in 34 B.C., built on a spur of Mount Taurus, commanding a distant view of the Euphrates valley, a sepulchral monument on which, side by side with the images of his ancestral gods, he set the scheme of his nativity figured on a large bas-relief,[3] because his life had realised all the promises of this horoscope. The cities of Syria often stamp on their coins certain signs of the zodiac to mark the fact that they stood under their patronage. If princes and cities thus acknowledged the authority of astrology, we may imagine what was the power of this scientific theology in the temples. We may say that in the Alexandrine age it permeated the whole of Semitic paganism.

But in the empire of the Seleucids alongside of this "Chaldaism," if I may venture to use the term, Hellenism had established itself in a commanding position. Above the old native beliefs the doctrines of Stoicism in particular exercised dominion over men's minds. It has often been observed that the masters of the Stoic school are for the most part Orientals. Zeno himself was born at Kition in the island of Cyprus. Among his successors Chrysippus and others belonged to Tarsus in Cilicia. Diogenes of Babylon, Posidonius of Apamea, Antipater of Tyre—to mention only the leading representatives

[1] See below, Lecture IV, p. 69 sqq.
[2] Diodorus Sic., ii, 31.
[3] Humann and Puchstein, *Reise in Nord Syrien und Klein Asien*, Berlin, 1890, pl. XL.

of these doctrines—were all Syrians. In a certain sense it may
be said that Stoicism was a Semitic philosophy. Given the fact
that it was always the first care of this school to reconcile itself
with established cults, it is *a priori* certain that Oriental star-
worship did not remain foreign to its system. Had we a more
precise knowledge of Asiatic civilisation during the Hellenistic
period, we should be able to estimate more exactly what Zeno
and, above all, his disciples owed to Chaldean theology and
what it owed to them. We have already touched upon this
point.[1] As it is, we cannot follow the development of this movement of ideas, which was definitively to introduce astrology
together with star-worship into the philosophy of the Stoa.
The thinker who is almost the sole representative we have of
these syncretic tendencies, despite the fact that they must
certainly have shown themselves long before him and abun-
dantly around him, is Posidonius of Apamea.

Of the man himself we know almost nothing. Born at
Apamea in the valley of the Orontes about 135 B.C., after
long travels in pursuit of his studies, which took him as far as
Gades (Cadiz), he settled in the island of Rhodes, whither his
teaching attracted large numbers of Greeks and Romans, and
he died at the age of eighty-four after an active career which
filled the whole of the first half of the first century. Was he a
pure Syrian, like Porphyry and Iamblichus in later times, or a
descendant of the Macedonian conquerors? Was his mother-
tongue Greek or Aramaic? We should like to know, but we
are in total ignorance about the surroundings amid which this
great man grew up; we know nothing of his society, nothing
even of his education, except that he was the pupil of the Stoic
Panætius.

But it is clear that this master, who in his time exercised a
real intellectual sovereignty, owed it above all to the extent of
his knowledge and the largeness of his comprehension. A
native of the very heart of Syria, but naturalised as a Rhodian,
Posidonius represented in all its fulness the alliance of Semitic
tradition with Greek thought. He was the great intermediary
and mediator not only between Romans and Hellenes, but

[1] See above, Lecture II, p. 40.

between East and West. Brought up on Plato and Aristotle, he was equally versed in Asiatic astrology and demonology. If he is Greek in the constructive power of his speculative genius, in the harmonious flow of his copious and highly-coloured style, his genius remained Oriental in the singular combination of the most exact science with a fervent mysticism. More of a theologian than a philosopher, in mind more learned than critical, he made all human knowledge conspire to the building up of a great system, the coping of which was enthusiastic adoration of the God who permeates the universal organism. In this vast syncretism all superstitions, popular or sacerdotal, soothsaying, divination, magic, find their place and their justification; but above all it was due to him that astrology entered into a coherent explanation of the world, acceptable to the most enlightened intellects, and that it was solidly based on a general theory of nature, from which it was to remain henceforth inseparable.

The almost total loss of the works of Posidonius prevents us from appreciating, save in an imperfect manner, the persuasive force of his teaching. But the echo of his words resounded far through the Roman dominion, where his authority balanced that of Epicurus. In his school at Rhodes he had long been the master of the masters of the world,—Pompey listened to him, Cicero attended his lectures,—and his influence on the development of later theology was immense in several directions. His pupil, Cicero, has frequent reminiscences of his teaching and translates his ideas into Latin. The symbolism of Philo the Jew is often inspired by his picturesque eloquence. Still later his ideas pass into and spread throughout the Stoic school—we see them, for instance, in the works of Seneca,—and they are echoed in the treatises of the astrologers of the imperial age.

The most striking of the literary productions which he inspired is the *Astronomics* of the so-called Manilius, a writer of whom we know absolutely nothing, not even his name, which is corrupt in the manuscripts, but who was in his own way a genuine poet: A work of remarkable inspiration, where the brilliance of the descriptions blooms in the wilderness of a dry "mathematic," where a passionate enthusiasm for the marvels of science makes us forget that this science is false, where lofty intellectual ambitions and an unbounded confidence in the power of reason are combined with a blind and puerile credulity which accepts all predictions derived from the stars,—this work reveals to us better than any other the grandeur of such a system of the world as that conceived by Posidonius and the attraction which was exercised by this learned cosmology, sustained by a mystic faith in astrology, the revealer of the future.

The poem is dedicated to Tiberius, who perhaps suggested its composition, and some have proposed to see in it "the expression of the official religion of the age." [1] Obviously the first Cæsars, even more than the old republican aristocracy, among whom Posidonius counted so many disciples, would be inclined to adopt the ideas of one who broke with the old national particularism, in order to include the worships of all races in one vast synthesis, and appeared to give to the united Empire the formula of the theology of the future. Characteristically enough, Augustus as well as Tiberius had already been converted to astrology, and we shall see how the later princes granted an official protection to sidereal religion.

With the same movement of ideas, which was initiated or represented by Posidonius, was connected the revival of a strange sect, that of the Neo-Pythagoreans, which re-appeared in the East during the first half of the first century before our era. Although by its ideal of religious life it professed to connect itself with the old Pythagorean mysticism, its doctrine owes more to the theories developed by Posidonius, especially in his commentary on the *Timaeus*, and it borrowed much, either through the medium of the great Syrian or even directly, from Oriental religions. A marked dualism, which contrasts the soul with the body, and, as a consequence, a moral asceticism, a doctrine of the eternity of the universe and of the influence of the stars on the constant changes of the sublunary world, a belief in airy demons who defile and torment mankind, but above all—and this is the central point and the core of its

[1] Gardthausen, *Augustus und seine Zeit*, p. 1131.

dogmatic system—a symbolism of numbers, to which is attributed an active force and a mystic power, all these essential features indicate a singularly close connection between Neo-Pythagorism and "Chaldean" theology. It is characteristic that the man who first revived at Rome the old South-Italian philosophy, Nigidius Figulus, the friend of Cicero, displays a curious interest in magic and in occult lore, and an ardent devotion to astrology, and that he was the first to expound in Latin the significance of the "barbaric sphere," that is to say, a series of constellations not recognised by the Greek astronomers but adopted in Oriental uranography.[1]

But these groups of cultured theosophists addressed themselves only to limited circles of "intellectuals." In a general way the new sidereal religion was from the first welcomed by the upper classes: it was cultivated by the aristocracy both of blood and of intellect. If it had continued to be preached only by polytheistic theorists, it would have remained, as in Greece, the exclusive preserve of a few speculative minds. Even the inspiration of a semi-official poet like Manilius would hardly have won for it the favour of the imperial court. And yet it achieved a widespread popularity. Its influence over the masses it did not owe to a literary diffusion, whatever may have been the success of certain romances which were inspired by it, such as the life of Apollonius by Philostratus and, still more, the *Ethiopics* of Heliodorus. It had in its service other missionaries, whose active propagandism spread it through the mixed populace of the towns as well as among the hosts of slaves who tilled the country estates. These popular propagandists were the clergy and the devotees of Oriental cults.

❧   ❧

Towards the commencement of our era, when the peace and unity of the ancient world was assured by the foundation of the Empire, began the development of this great religious movement which little by little was to orientalise Roman paganism. The gods of the nations of the Levant imposed themselves, one after another, on the West. Cybele and Attis were transported

[1] See F. Boll, *Sphaera*, Leipsic, 1903.

from Phrygia, Isis and Serapis travelled thither from Alexandria. Merchants, soldiers, and slaves brought the Baals of Syria and Mithra, an immigrant from the heart of Persia. We have attempted in another volume to show in what respects each of these foreign cults enriched the creeds of Rome.[1] The point which I desire to emphasise here, is that all of them, no matter what their origin, were influenced in different degrees by astrology and star-worship. These doctrines, as we have seen, grew up among the temples of Syria and Egypt, and transformed the theology of these countries more and more. Originally the mysteries of Isis and Serapis, established under the first Ptolemy, allowed them only a limited place, but in the time of Nero his teacher Chæremon, a priest of Alexandria and a Stoic philosopher, re-discovered in the religion of Egypt the worship of the powers of nature and, in particular, of the stars, and found again in prayer a means of rescuing men from the fatality which the influence of the heavenly bodies imposed upon them. Even in Asia Minor, where the sidereal cult is adventitious and recent, a member of a considerable family of Phrygian prelates is found celebrating in verse the sidereal divination which enabled him to publish far and wide infallible predictions. Attis, the Anatolian deity of vegetation, ended by becoming a solar god, just like Serapis, the Baals, and Mithra. In very early times, even in Mesopotamia, star-worship was imposed upon Persian Mazdaism, which was still a collection of traditions and rites rather than a body of doctrines, and a set of abstruse dogmas came to be super-imposed on the naturalistic myths of the Iranians. The mysteries of Mithra imported into Europe this composite theology, off-spring of the intercourse between Magi and Chaldeans; and the signs of the zodiac, the symbols of the planets, the emblems of the elements, appear time after time on the bas-reliefs, mosaics, and paintings of their subterranean temples. We find one of the members of their clergy proclaimed in his epitaph at Milan *studiosus astrologiae*.[2] The priests of the Persian god and

---

[1] *The Oriental Religions in Roman Paganism*, Chicago (Open Court Publishing Company), 1911.
[2] *Corp. Inscr. Lat.*, v, 5893.

those of the so-called "Jupiters" of Syria contributed largely
to the triumph of this pseudo-science, which towards the age of
the Severi acquired an almost undisputed supremacy even in
the Latin world.

Here it no longer presents itself as a learned theory taught by
mathematicians, but as a sacred doctrine revealed to the adepts
of exotic cults, which have all assumed the form of mysteries.
The doctrine which is thus communicated to the initiated in
the dim light of temples, undoubtedly remained more sacerdotal than, for instance, the *Tetrabiblos* of Ptolemy, a dry
didactic treatise which could never have fostered any devotion.
Here more room was left for mythology, mysticism, ethics, and
superstition. This theology, however, had not escaped the
prevailing ascendancy of Greek philosophy, any more than had
the ideas of the most learned casters of nativities,—this is a fact
which research has succeeded in proving. In reality these
mysteries, which professed to be the depositaries of an ancient
tradition imported from the Far East, constantly modified
their teaching, in order to adapt it to altered times and environ-
ments; and if the wisdom which they revealed was always
regarded as divine, it nevertheless varied remarkably in the
course of ages and admitted ideas entirely foreign to its original
content. This was a necessary consequence of the close union
of learning and belief which, as we have said, characterises
Oriental religions. They were always the expression of a given
conception of the world, which determined the relations of
heaven and earth and the duties of the faithful towards the
gods. Hence they were bound to change in conformity with
the evolution of physical or metaphysical ideas. If Greek
thought could receive certain impulses or suggestions from
the temples of Syria and Egypt, it invaded them in turn as a
conqueror: and Stoicism in particular certainly gave to them
more than it received from them. The great intellectual
movement of which Posidonius was not so much the initiator
as the most illustrious representative, undoubtedly combined
devotion and philosophy, but it also introduced philosophy
into devotion. The learned and mystic system of doctrine, which
Manilius and others preached under Tiberius, imposed itself

on all Western paganism in the course of the following centuries; and we may say, making allowance for certain modifications, that this half-scientific, half-religious system, which was established in the Alexandrine period, continued to be the theology of the mysteries up to the time of their disappearance, even after the advent of Neo-Platonism.

As a characteristic production of this medley of ideas may be quoted those *Chaldean Oracles*,[1] whose origin is still a mystery, but which appear to have been compiled in the second century of our era. In these works of fantastic mysticism, in which the whole Neo-Platonic school saw the revelation of supreme wisdom, ancient beliefs of Semitic star-worship are combined with Hellenic theories. They are to Babylon what the Hermetic literature is to Egypt.

Thus the triumph of Oriental religions was simultaneously the triumph of astral religion, but to secure recognition by all pagan peoples, it needed an official sanction. The influence which it had acquired among the populace, was finally assured when the emperors lent it an interested support. That apotheosis by which from the beginning of the principate deceased princes were raised to the stars, is inspired both in form and spirit by Asiatic doctrines. We have seen that already Augustus and especially Tiberius allowed themselves to be converted to the ideas of the disciples of Posidonius. But they remained hostile to the popular forms of foreign worships, at least in their capital. Their ideal, which was entirely political, is the restoration of the old Roman faith and respect for the purely practical cult of the city. But in proportion as Cæsarism became more and more transformed into absolute monarchy, it tended more and more to lean for support on the Oriental clergy. These priests, loyal to the traditions of the Achæmenids and the Pharaohs, preached doctrines which tended to elevate sovereigns above mankind, and they supplied the emperors with a dogmatic justification of their despotism. For the old

[1] *Λόγια Χαλδαϊκά.*

principle of the sovereignty of the people, the original form of Cæsarism, was substituted a reasoned belief in supernatural influences. The emperor is the image of the Sun on earth, like him invincible and eternal (*invictus*, *aeternus*), as his official title declares. Already in the eyes of the Babylonians the Sun was the royal planet, and it is he that in Rome continues to give to his chosen ones the virtues of sovereignty, and destines them for the throne from the time of their appearance on earth. He remains in close communion with them, he is their companion (*comes*) and their congener, for they are united by community of nature. It may be said that they are consubstantial; and in the third century the monarch was worshipped as "god and master by right of birth" (*deus et dominus natus*), who had descended from heaven by grace of the Sun, and by his grace will reascend thither again after death. The idea that the monarch's soul, at the moment when destiny caused it to descend to this world, received from the Star of the day its sovereign power, led to the inference that he participated in the might of this divinity, and was its representative on earth. Thus it is noticeable that the princes who proclaimed most loudly their autocratic pretensions, a Domitian or a Commodus, were also those who most openly favoured Oriental cults.

These cults attained the zenith of their power when the advent of the Severi brought them the support of a half-Syrian Court. For nearly half a century, from A.D. 193 to 235, the Empire was governed by a family of Emesa, an ancient sacerdotal state, where on the edge of the Syrian desert rose the splendid temple of Elagabalus. Intelligent and ambitious princesses, Julia Domna, Sohæmias, Mæsa, and Mammæa, whose intellectual ascendancy was so considerable, became missionaries of their national religion. Officials of all ranks, senators and officers, rivalled each other in devotion to the gods who protected their sovereigns and were protected by them. You all know the bold proclamation of A.D. 218 which set upon the throne a boy of fourteen years, priest of Elagabalus, whose name he bore. The Greeks named him Heliogabalus in order to recall the solar character of this god. To this barbarous divinity, hitherto rather obscure, he sought to give the primacy over all the others. Ancient authors relate with indignation how this crowned priest desired to elevate the black stone of his god, a rude idol brought from Emesa, to the rank of sovereign divinity of the Empire, subordinating the entire pantheon of antiquity to *Sol Invictus Elagabal*, as he is termed in inscriptions. The attempt of Heliogabalus to establish in heaven a kind of solar monotheism corresponding to the monarchy that ruled on earth, was doubtless too violent, tactless, and premature: it miscarried and provoked the assassination of its author.

But it corresponded to the aspirations of the day and it was renewed half a century later, this time with complete success. In 274, Aurelian was inspired with the same idea, when he created a new cult of the "Invincible Sun." Worshipped in a splendid temple, served by pontiffs who were raised to the level of the ancient pontiffs of Rome, celebrated every fourth year by magnificent games, *Sol Invictus* was definitively promoted to the highest rank in the divine hierarchy and became the official protector of the Sovereigns and of the Empire. The country in which Aurelian discovered the model which he sought to reproduce was Syria, where he had won a decisive victory over the famous queen Zenobia: he placed in his new sanctuary the images of Bel and Helios, which he captured at Palmyra. In establishing this new State cult, Aurelian in reality proclaimed the dethronement of the old Roman idolatry and the accession of Semitic Sun-worship.

With Constantius Chlorus (A.D. 305) there ascended the throne a solar dynasty which, connecting itself with Claudius II Gothicus, a votary of the worship of Apollo, professed to have *Sol Invictus* as its special protector and ancestor. Even the Christian emperors, Constantine and Constantius, did not altogether forget the pretensions which they could derive from so illustrious a descent, and the last pagan who occupied the throne of the Cæsars, Julian the Apostate, has left us a discourse in which, in the style of a subtle theologian and a fervent devotee, he justifies the adoration of the King Star, of whom he considered himself the spiritual son and heaven-sent champion.

If in conclusion we survey at a glance the whole course of the expansion which we have tried to describe, we shall be struck with the power of this sidereal theology, founded on ancient beliefs of Chaldean astrologers, transformed in the Hellenistic age under the twofold influence of astronomic discoveries and Stoic thought, and promoted, after becoming a pantheistic Sun-worship, to the rank of official religion of the Roman Empire. Preached on the one hand by men of letters and by men of science in centres of culture, diffused on the other hand among the bulk of the people by the servitors of Semitic, Persian or Egyptian gods, it is finally patronised by the emperors, who find in it at once a form of worship suitable for all their subjects and a justification of their autocratic pretensions.

In this way the astrological conception of life and of the world permeated the whole of society, and in particular produced a revolution in the beliefs of the Latin world. Despite all the speculations of metaphysicians, the masses had remained on the whole true to the old idolatry of the Republican period. Oriental theology led to the prevalence of a more lofty idea of God. In the declining days of antiquity the common creed of all pagans came to be a scientific pantheism, in which the infinite power of the divinity that pervaded the universe was revealed by all the elements of nature. In the following lectures we shall have to examine more closely this conception of the world, the theology which was bound up with it, and the moral and eschatological ideas which were derived from it.

LECTURE IV. *Theology*

Posidonius defined man as "the beholder and expounder of heaven."[1] Nature itself—the ancients vied with each other in insisting on this point—destined him to contemplate the sky and to observe its perpetual motions. Other animals bend towards the earth, but man proudly raises his eyes to the stars, —this is an idea which we find repeated time after time. His eye, the marvel of the human body, tiny mirror in which immensity is reflected, gateway of the soul open towards the infinite, follows from here below the distant evolutions of the celestial armies. The old astronomers, who did not use the telescope, marvelled at the power of the eye, and the ancients expressed their astonishment at the range of vision which reached the remotest constellations. They give it the pre-eminence over all the other senses, for the eyes are to them the intermediaries between the sidereal gods and human reason. Struck by the light from on high, the power of sight devotes itself to following the motions of these radiant bodies, which move above us. It ascertains that the course of the sun, which occasions the changes of the seasons, the phases of the moon, the rising and the setting of the fixed stars, even the march of the planets which appear to be wandering stars, are all regulated by immutable laws, and are reproduced in accordance with invariable periods of time. In heaven there are never derangements or errors, there nothing moves without design. Reason, reflecting on the marvellous phenomena which are perceived by the eye, realises that they cannot be due to chance or to the action of a blind force, but recognises that they are ruled by a divine intelligence. The ceaseless harmony of movements so diverse is inconceivable without the intervention of a guiding Providence. The stars themselves prove to us

[1] Capelle, *Die Schrift von der Welt*, Leipzig, 1895, p. 6 [534], n. 4. "*Contemplatorem caeli.*" "*Οὐ μόνον θεατὴν ἀλλὰ καὶ ἐξηγητήν.*"

their divinity so clearly that to fail to see it is to be incapable of seeing anything. Nobody could deny to the heavenly bodies the possession of reason without being himself destitute of it: that at least is the opinion of Cicero.[1] The view of the starry heaven thus led to astronomy and to philosophy, which are the queens of the sciences, the one in the domain of the visible, the other in the domain of ideas; and the study of these is the noblest employment to which man can put his faculties.

We have seen that since the days of Plato and Aristotle, and even earlier,[2] Greek thinkers proved the divinity of the stars by the character of their movements, and in a general way all metaphysicians point to the order of nature as proving the existence of God. Voltaire himself in the *Philosophical Dictionary* uses expressions on this subject which would not have been disowned by the ancients. But what characterises ancient ideas is the fact that they closely connect belief in the gods with observation of the sky. Astronomy here serves as an introduction to theology. This sidereal religion, developed by an erudite clergy, has always retained the stamp of its learned origin.

❧   ❧

The essential quality of these sidereal gods, the one most frequently insisted upon, is that they are everlasting. We have seen that astronomy had led the old Chaldeans to this notion.[3] The invariability of the revolutions of the heavenly bodies led to the conclusion that they were eternal. The stars unceasingly pursue their never-ending course; arrived at the limit of their path, they resume without pause the race already run, and the cycles of years, in accordance with which their movements take place, are prolonged to infinity in the past, and continue to infinity in the future. Thus a clergy of astronomers necessarily conceived the gods of heaven, as being "the masters of eternity," or "those whose name is praised to all eternity,"—these titles are constantly bestowed in inscriptions on the Syrian Baals. The stars which the Syrians worshipped did not die, like

[1] Cic., *Nat. Deorum*, ii, 21, § 56.
[2] See above, Lecture II, p. 23.
[3] See above, Lecture I, p. 18.

Osiris in Egypt, or Attis in Asia Minor: each time they seemed to sink, they were born again to a new life, always unconquerable. This theological notion penetrated with astrology into Roman paganism. As often as a dedication is found to a *deus Aeternus*, it refers to a sidereal, most frequently a Syrian, god. The epithet *aeternus* completes and explains that of *invictus*, which, like the former, is applied to the stars in general, and specially to the Sun. These celestial powers always issue triumphantly from their strife with darkness; unceasingly menaced, they have been, are, and shall be ever victorious.

It is a remarkable fact that it is not until the second century of our era that this qualifying epithet *aeternus* comes into use in ritual at the same time as the cult of the god Heaven (*Caelus*) spreads. In vain had philosophers long set the First Cause beyond the limitations of time: their theories had not made impression on the popular mind, nor had they succeeded in modifying the traditional formulary of liturgies. For the multitude, divinities remained beings more beautiful, more vigorous, more powerful than men, but born like them and preserved only from decay and death. Semitic priests popularised throughout the Roman world the idea that God is without beginning and without end, and so contributed, side by side with Jewish proselytism, to invest with the authority of a religious dogma what had hitherto been but a metaphysical theory.

The importance attached to this idea enables us to understand that it was applied even to gods living upon the earth, in whom an image or manifestation of the sun was seen. The emperors, whose soul has descended to earth from heaven above, and is to re-ascend thither after death, are called, from the second century onwards, not only *invicti* but *aeterni*, like the stars to which they are united by identity of nature. This expression was introduced into the official vocabulary, and ultimately a sovereign was addressed as "Your Eternity," almost as naturally as we say "Your Majesty," although that epithet, applied to the short-lived princes who, in the third century, flit across the throne like shadows across a screen, seems almost cruelly ironical.

This, however, is but a political caricature of a great religious idea,—an idea which appealed to the imagination, and which poetry also adopted. Manilius [1] contrasts the permanence of the heavens with the frailty of earthly things:

Thrones have perished, peoples passed from dominion to slavery, from captivity to empire, but the same months of the year have always brought up on the horizon the same stars. All things that are subject to death are also subject to change, the years glide away, and lands become unrecognisable, each century transforms the features of nations, but Heaven remains invariable, and preserves all its parts; the flight of time adds nothing to them, nor does age take aught from them. It will remain the same for ever, because for ever it has been the same. Thus it appeared to the eyes of our forefathers, thus will our descendants behold it. It is God, for it is unchangeable throughout the ages.

Men did not stop there, but separating eternity from the stars and from heaven, whose loftiest quality it was, they adored that eternity itself as a divinity. Here is not a mere abstraction, like Equity or Clemency or one of the many other abstractions which the Romans had conceived and fervently worshipped, notwithstanding the fact that they figured *Aeternitas* on their coins. The path which led to this worship is more intricate, and its beginnings go back to a very early stage of thought. Time, when this notion, which is lacking among many savages, appeared, was not defined as a conception of the reason, or in Kant's phrase, "*a priori* form of conception." This is a being who has an existence *per se*, who is even regarded sometimes as a material body, and who is endowed with an activity of his own. "Zeno," says Cicero,[2] "attributed a divine power (*vis divina*) to the stars, but also to the years, the months, and the seasons." We have here a very ancient belief, which is found for instance in Egypt. The magic idea of a power superior to man is connected, from the very beginning, with the notation of time Calendars had a religious before acquiring a secular significance: their original object was not to secure the measurement of the gliding moments, but to indicate the

[1] Manil., *Astron.*, i, 495 sqq.
[2] Cic., *Nat. Deor.*, ii, 63 (=Zenon. fr. 165 von Arnim).

recurrence of propitious or unpropitious dates separated by periodic intervals. It is an empirical fact that the return of fixed moments is associated with the appearance of certain phenomena: it is easy to believe that the one is the cause of the other. They have therefore a peculiar efficacy, a sacred character.[1] Astronomy fixed the duration of these periods with an ever-increasing accuracy: it not only distinguished the sequence of days and nights, but also that of the months, corresponding to the revolutions of the moon, and that of the years, corresponding to those of the sun. Its progress led to a division of the day into two periods of twelve hours each. All these durations continued to be regarded as having a definite influence, as being endowed with a magic potency, and astrology sought to codify these activities, by placing each division of time under the protection of a star in its system of "chronocratories."

When the idea of an Eternity arose, more vast than the sum-total of years and centuries, it was regarded likewise as a divinity. "General opinion," says Proclus,[2] "makes the Hours goddesses and the Month a god, and their worship has been handed on to us: we say also that the Day and the Night are deities, and the gods themselves have taught us how to call upon them. Does it not necessarily follow that Time also should be a god, seeing that it includes at once months and hours, days and nights?"

In fact infinity of Time was elevated to the dignity of Supreme Cause not only by individual thinkers, but by Oriental cults. You all know by name Zervan Akarana, "Time Unlimited," which a sect of Persian Magi regarded as the First Principle. This doctrine, which was developed in Mesopotamia, was adopted by the mysteries of Mithra and passed with them into the West, where this god was represented in the form of a monster with the head of a lion, to indicate that he devours all things. As might have been expected, the worship of Time was there closely combined with that of "the eternal Heaven" (*Caelus aeternus*), whose revolutions marked its

[1] See above, Lecture I, p. 19.
[2] Proclus, *In Timæum*, 248 D.

everlasting course, and, as the master of all things, it was sometimes identified with Destiny, whose irresistible activity was
exerted to produce the endless motion of the stars.

Each portion of Infinity brings on some propitious or unpropitious movement of the heavens, which is anxiously
watched, and these motions incessantly modify the earthly
world. The Centuries and the Years, each subject to the influence of a star or a constellation, the Seasons which are
related to the four winds and to the four cardinal points, the
twelve Months over which the signs of the zodiac preside,
the Day and the Night, the twelve Hours, are all personified
and deified, as being the authors of all the changes of the
universe.

The allegorical figures invented by astrological cults to
represent these abstractions came into common use under the
Empire. This symbolism did not even die out with idolatry:
it was adopted by Christianity, in spite of the fact that it was in
reality contrary to its spirit, and up to the Middle Ages these
symbols of the fallen gods were reproduced *ad infinitum* in
sculpture, mosaics, and miniatures, and it may be said that
the old superstitions of the Chaldeans are still perpetuated by
modern art.

Like the divisions of Time, numbers were divine for a
similar reason. The ancients said that they had been revealed
to mankind by the motions of the stars.[1] In fact the progress of
mathematics must often have been a result of the progress of
astronomy, and the former participated in the sacred character
of the latter. Certain numerals were thus considered for
astronomical reasons as endowed with an especial potency:
seven and nine, which are the fourth and the third part of the
month, seven again and twelve, because they correspond to
the planets and to the signs of the zodiac, three hundred and
sixty, because that was the—approximate—number of days in
the year. To these figures was attributed a peculiar efficacy;
thus it was necessary in magical incantations to repeat the
operative formula for a given number of times in order that it
might produce the desired effect. Mathematics also entered

[1] See above, Lecture I, p. 18; II, p. 29.

largely into astrological divination,—*mathematici* is in Latin a synonym of *Chaldaei*,—and they served as a foundation or a pretext for a subtle and extravagant symbolism. Thus very often a name is replaced by a numerical equivalent, that is, by the sum-total of its letters considered as figures and added together. But despite these uses and abuses, connected with sidereal religion or, at least, superstition, there is a great difference between numbers and the divisions of Time: the former might be sacred, they could never be deified, they were not worshipped, nor were artistic representations of them imagined.

What has been said brings out the importance attached by the adepts of star-worship to the idea of divine eternity,—an importance shown by the fact that some had actually made it the supreme principle of their religion. But there was another divine attribute correlative to the former. The stars are not only eternal gods, but also universal, their power is unlimited in space as in time. Already in Syria the Baals, who had become solar deities, bore the title of *Mar'olam*, which may be translated "Lord of the Universe" as well as "Lord of Eternity," and men undoubtedly liked to claim for them this double quality.[1] With earthly *genii* or demons, who protected definite spots, were contrasted the celestial gods, who are "catholic." This word, which was to have such a great destiny, was at first merely an astrological term: it denoted activities which are not limited to individuals, nor to particular events, but apply to the whole human race and to the entire earth.

Everything is, in fact, subject to the changes brought about by the revolutions of the stars. All the events of this world are determined by sidereal influences. The transformations of nature, like the dispositions and actions of man, are due to the fatal energies which reside in the sky. Hence necessarily follows not only the idea of the universality, but also that of the omnipotence, of the sidereal deities. The Semitic cults

[1] *Religions orientales*, 2d edition, Paris, 1909, p. 375, n. 80 (Engl. translation, p. 258, n. 80).

spread throughout the Latin world the conception of the absolute, unlimited sovereignty of God over the earth. Apuleius of Madaura calls the Syrian goddess "*omnipotens et omniparens,*" all-powerful and all-producing.

But here we must make a distinction: if all the gods are equally everlasting, all cannot be universal and omnipotent in the same degree. Undoubtedly Destiny holds sovereign sway over the whole world, and the celestial orbs by their combined movements are the authors of all that was, and is, and is to come. But this unlimited power only belongs properly to the *ensemble* of the cosmic harmony. It resides in the Whole regarded as divine, it manifests itself to a greater or less degree in its different parts. Perhaps you remember the opening of Dante's *Il Paradiso*:

> La gloria di colui che tutto muove
> Per l' universo penetra e risplende
> In una parte più e meno altrove.
> Nel ciel che più della sua luce prende,
> Fu' io . . .

The poet of the Middle Ages is only expressing here an astrological notion. The starry heaven is the principal seat of the divine energy and light which are spread throughout the world. But all the stars have not an equal share of its power: only some among them, or even one among them, can properly be called "catholic" and omnipotent ($\pi\alpha\nu\tau o\kappa\rho\acute{\alpha}\tau\omega\rho$). We proceed to pass in review these various divinities.

      ❧   ☙

The highest of these gods is Heaven ($O\mathring{v}\rho\alpha\nu\acute{o}\varsigma$, *Caelus*), "*Summus ipse deus,*" says Cicero,[1] "*arcens et continens ceteros,*" that is to say, the heaven of the fixed stars, which embraces all the other spheres. The divine Power which there resides, and which causes it to move, was sometimes in the West identified with Bel,—that is to say, with Zeus,—and in Latin lands was invoked under the title of "*Optimus Maximus Caelus Aeternus Iupiter.*" The movement of this heaven was a continuous

---

[1] Cicer., *Somn. Scipionis*, c. 4.

revolution, not a motion forwards and backwards like that of the planets, and, assigning a moral sense to the word ἀπλανής, men said that since it did not *wander* or *err*, therefore it was not subject to error, and that this infallibility was a proof of its divinity. Certain theologians, associating this with infinite Time, represented Heaven as the supreme power of the world.

The vast orb of the sky was deified in its whole, and in its parts. Its two portions, alternately dark and luminous, were worshipped under the form of the Dioscuri. The sons of Tyndareus, according to the Greek legend, shared in turn life and death, and they became in the eyes of theologians the personification of the two hemispheres.

But each of the constellations, each star which glittered in the eternal vault, was equally divine. Each had its myth. As we have already said,[1] the traditional figures which we reproduce on our celestial charts, are the fossil remains of a luxuriant mythological vegetation. The sidereal monsters, to which potent virtues were attributed, were the residuum of a number of forgotten beliefs. Worship of animals had been abandoned in temples, but the Lion, the Bull, the Eagle, the Fishes, which Oriental imagination had recognised in the capricious grouping of the stars, continued to be considered sacred. Old totems of Semitic tribes or of Egyptian nomes survived in the form of constellations. Heterogeneous elements, borrowed from all the religions of the East, were combined in ancient uranography, and in the power attributed to the phantoms which it conjured up was repeated the echo of old-fashioned worships, which frequently remain unknown to us.

Then came the Greeks, who professed to piece these celestial beings on to their national religion. They succeeded in adorning the sky without troubling themselves very much to distinguish their own inventions from those which they received from a foreign tradition. "Catasterism," that is "translation to the stars," was a convenient method of giving an astronomical termination to ancient fables. Thus poetical tales, which were only half believed, represented fabulous heroes and even members of human society as living on high in the form of

[1] See above, Lecture I, p. 11.

glittering constellations. There Perseus found Andromeda again, and the centaur Chiron, who is none other than the Archer, fraternised with Orion, the gigantic hunter. "The Ram was the famous ram with the Golden Fleece which had carried off Phrixus and Helle over the sea and had let the maiden fall into the waves of the Hellespont. It might also be that which was the subject of the dispute between Atreus and Thyestes, or again it might be the ram which guided the thirsty company of Bacchus to the wells of the oasis of Ammon." [1]

But this patch-work assemblage of heroes, animals, and sacred objects was scarcely worshipped save *en bloc*. Particular veneration was bestowed on twelve constellations to which the most potent influence over destiny was attributed, namely, the twelve signs of the zodiac. Astrological treatises are full of details concerning their qualities; and their influence, which results sometimes from their astronomic nature, sometimes from the mythical character which was bestowed upon them, was exerted especially during the month over which each presided, and their images figure in large numbers on the monuments of pagan worship, particularly on those of the mysteries of Mithra. Further even than this, since each sign of the zodiac was divided into three decans, a god was imagined for each of these thirty-six compartments of the heaven.

Not only were the stars of heaven an object of worship, but also the subtle substance which lit their fires, the Ether which filled the lofty spaces of the heavens. Sacrifices were offered to it, or it was celebrated in hymns as the source of all brightness, and the worshippers even dedicated inscriptions to this pure and serene air that it might chase away the devastating hail.

Into the sphere of the fixed stars, which marks the bounds of the world, are fitted seven other spheres, those of the planets, which are, in order, Saturn, Jupiter, Mars, the Sun, Venus, Mercury, and the Moon. The qualities and influences which are attributed to them are due sometimes to astronomical motives. They are deduced from their apparent movements as discovered by observation. Saturn makes people apathetic and vacillating, because, being farthest from the earth, it appears

[1] Bouché–Leclercq, *Astrologie grecque*, p. 131.

to move most deliberately. But most frequently the reasons assigned are purely mythological. The planets, being identified with the divinities of Olympus, have borrowed their nature. Mars, Venus, Mercury, have a history known to all: the mere mention of their names is enough to explain their action: Venus needs must favour lovers, and Mercury assure success in business and swindling. This double conception of planetary divinities, of whom now one, now the other, displays the activities, favourable or destructive, which are attributed to them, corresponds to the hybrid origin of astrology, which pretends to be a science but always remained a creed, and is found again also, to a lesser degree, in the doctrines concerning fixed stars.

But, like the Olympians who were identified with them, the planetary gods are much the most powerful of all. Their positions in the sky, their reciprocal relations or, to use the technical term, *aspects*, have a decisive influence on all physical and moral phenomena of this world. They exercise a manifold patronage, more diverse and more extensive than that of the gods of Olympus and the saints of Paradise. They are the tutelary deities not only of the series of days,[1] but of that of the hours, and even of centuries and millenaries. To each was attached a plant, a metal, a stone, which derived miraculous powers from this special protection. Each presided over a period of life, a portion of the body, and a faculty of the soul, possessed a colour and a taste, corresponded to one of the vowels. These various relations in which they were supposed to stand to the whole of nature, afforded numerous opportunities for paying them worship. As we shall see in another lecture,[2] their worship was much more popular than that of the other sidereal gods, and their images are reproduced on monuments with much greater frequency.

Beneath the lowest sphere, that of the moon, the zones of the elements, are placed in tiers: the zones of fire, air, water, and earth. To these four principles, as well as to the constellations, the Greeks gave the name of στοιχεῖα, and the Chaldeans

[1] See below, Lecture V, p. 91.
[2] See Lecture V, p. 90.

already worshipped the one as well as the other. The influence of Oriental religions, like that of Stoic cosmology,
spread throughout the West the worship of these four bodies,
believed to be elements, whose infinite variety of combinations
gave rise to all perceptible phenomena. In the mysteries of
Mithra, a group, frequently reproduced, in which a lion
represented fire, a bowl water, and a serpent the earth, figured
emblematically the strife of these gods, at the same time kindly
and hostile, which constantly devoured each other, and whose
perpetual opposition and transmutation brought about all the
changes of nature. By the end of the pagan period, the divinity
of these physical agents was a religious principle accepted by
all heathendom. Consequently, by a piquant contrast, the con-
ventional representations of these polymorphous substances,
which antique sculpture had rarely chiselled, were multiplied
at the very moment when Christianity was robbing them of their
sacred character.

These elements were not only deified: they were themselves
haunted by formidable powers; especially the zone of air,
which envelops the earth, was the chosen home of demons,
kindly or malignant beings, who occupied the middle space
and served as intermediaries between gods and men, superior
to the latter, inferior to the former.

There is, however, an essential difference between the powers
of this sublunary world—elements and demons—and the stars.
The former are subject to the activity of the latter, their various
manifestations are caused by the combined influence of the
heavenly bodies; to the latter alone belong constancy and
regularity; they alone serve for the purposes of scientific
divination.

To sum up, then, this long catalogue, astrological paganism
deified the active principles which move all celestial and
terrestrial bodies. Water, fire, earth, the sea, and the blast of
the winds, but above all the luminous heavens of the fixed stars
and planets revealed the boundless power of the God who filled
all nature. But this pantheism no longer naïvely regarded this

nature as peopled by capricious spirits and unregulated powers. Having become scientific, it conceived the gods as cosmic energies, the providential action of which is ordered in a harmonious system.

Oriental theologians developed the idea that the world forms a trinity; it is three in one and one in three; it is made up of the sphere of the fixed stars, regarded as not resolvable into parts, of the seven spheres of the planets and of the earth, starting from the moon. According to some of these theologians, each of the inferior worlds received a portion of its power from the superior worlds and shared in their energy, and the source of all force and all virtue resided in the highest sphere, one and indivisible, which regulated the movements of all the other parts of the universe.

But this is not the theory which triumphed in the Roman empire. Rather it was supposed that the motive power, which set in motion all the cosmic organism, came from the Sun, and thus the Sun was raised to the rank of a Supreme God.[1] This Sun-worship was the logical result of a paganism steeped in erudition, which had become a religious form of cosmology. Renan[2] once observed: "The life of our planet has its real source in the sun. All force is a transformation of the sun. Before religion had gone so far as to proclaim that God must be placed in the absolute and the ideal, that is to say, outside of the world, one cult only was reasonable and scientific, and that was the cult of the Sun." The worship of Sun and Moon preceded that of the other planets, and even when the system of "the Seven" was constructed by astronomy, a distinction was made between the great luminaries which preside over day and night and the five other wandering stars. But it is a remarkable fact that at first the primacy was assigned to the Moon. It was only by slow degrees that the ancients discovered the unequalled importance in the cosmic system as a whole of the heavenly body which gives us light and, to say the truth, they never attained to the fulness of the idea. Thus it is that, if we

[1] See my paper, *La Théologie solaire du Paganisme romain* (Mém. Acad. Inscr., xii). Paris, 1909.
[2] Renan, *Dialogues et Fragments philosophiques*, 1876, p. 168.

go back to the earliest historical times, we see that in Babylonia the principal god—for he was endowed with the male sex,—was the Moon, Sin, which regularly precedes Shamash, the Sun. This god preserved the chief place at Carrhæ in Osroëne and throughout a large part of Anatolia up to the time of the Roman Empire. The predominance of the worship of Men, as he was called in Asia Minor, is due to the persistence in this remote country of ancient ideas, elsewhere out of date.

In hot countries the sun is, above all, an enemy, against which men protect themselves, and the dwellers in the scorching plains of Mesopotamia preferred to the star whose burning heat inflamed the air, parched the land, and exhausted the body, that star whose gentle light illumined, without menacing, them. In the freshness of the night the Moon shed the wholesome dews, and her brightness, then as now, guided caravans across the desert. Everywhere her phases, obvious to all eyes, served to measure time before the duration of the year was known, and sacred calendars regulated religious ceremonies and civil life according to her course. When her face was hidden, a fearful portent was seen in this eclipse, and there was attributed to this powerful divinity a multitude of mysterious influences, the recollection of which survived in astrology and was indefinitely perpetuated in popular superstitions. To it also were attributed strange effects on the growth of plants and on the health of women. As is often the case, the goddess retained in common belief the power of which theology had robbed her. However, she was never entirely deprived of her authority. In Egypt in spite of very early attempts to establish the undivided sovereignty of the Sun Ra, in the end, in heaven as on earth, preference was given over single sovereignty to the joint power of sister and brother, of wife and husband, of Isis and Osiris. This dualism still inspires the Alexandrine mysteries of the epoch of the Ptolemies, and is reaffirmed in the theories of Egyptian astrologers who divided the supremacy over the other five planets between the "two eyes of heaven."

But among the Semitic peoples an erudite clergy, hereditarily devoted to the study of the starry sky, drew more boldly the religious conclusions of their scientific discoveries. Little by little

they established the primary importance of the sun in the
celestial mechanism, and they asserted its pre-eminence more
confidently in proportion as they understood it better.

Continually placing it farther and farther off in space, these
priests acquired a more and more correct idea of its formidable
dimensions. When they had studied its revolutions, they realised
what relations connected it with physical phenomena and with
the succession of the seasons. The final blow was struck at the
ancient prestige of the moon when it was discovered that she
shines with a borrowed or, as they said, a bastard light. Sun-
worship is essentially a learned cult: it grew with science itself,
and was definitely established at the period when the latter
attained its zenith in antiquity. At no other point does one
perceive more clearly the ties which, in the religions of the
East, united intellectual research with the evolution of belief.

According to the so-called "Chaldean" system, the sun, as
we have seen,[1] occupies the fourth rank in the series of planets.
Three are above it, Mars, Jupiter, and Saturn, and three below
it, Venus, Mercury, and the Moon. In other words, the Sun
moves in the midst of the heavenly spheres. It occupies the
central position among the seven circles of the universe.

The other planets appeared to revolve round it, or rather to
escort it, and astrologers delighted to point to the Royal Sun
($Βασιλεὺς$ $Ἥλιος$) advancing in the midst of his satellites, as
earthly princes, whose tutelar star he is, march encircled by
their guards.

Further, the "Chaldeans" had thought out an original
solution of a problem which caused much perplexity to ancient
astronomers, namely, that presented by the irregular courses
of the planets. They had observed that the apparent advances,
stoppages, and regressions of these latter were connected with
the revolutions of the sun,—in reality of the earth,—and they
had come to the conclusion that the sun governed their movements: the sun was as it were the chorus-leader who directed
the rhythmic evolutions of the wandering stars. It not only
drew in its course Mercury and Venus which, as had been
ascertained, were never more than a short distance from it, but

[1] See above, this Lecture, p. 66.

it also regulated the movements of the three superior planets, and acted upon them by the force of its heat in much the same way as upon terrestrial vapours, which it caused to ascend or descend. According to the position which it occupies relatively to them, it impels them forwards, arrests them, or drives them backwards; and this it does mechanically, exerting its power, like every astrological influence, according to certain angles or "aspects."

Berosus made a particular application of this same theory to the phases of the moon, and other Chaldeans extended this explanation to the movements of comets. They even went so far as to make the revolutions of the fixed stars depend upon the sun. The essential idea on which all these doctrines were based is that the sun in virtue of its intense heat possesses a power of alternate repulsion and attraction, which according to its distance, or the direction of its rays, now drives the heavenly bodies away from it, and now draws them towards it, —unique focus of energy which causes them all to move. This mechanical theory, which contains a sort of anticipation of the doctrine of universal gravitation and of the heliocentric system, was bound to serve as the basis of a whole learned theology.

For, as we have said, in the eyes of Chaldean astronomers the fixed stars, and above all the planets, are the authors of all the phenomena of the universe, and nothing here below is produced save in virtue of their combined activities. That, then, which rules the complicated play of their revolutions and their aspects, will be the arbiter of destiny, the master of all nature. Placed at the centre of the great cosmic organism, it animates the whole of it, as the heart supports human life, and both in scientific treatises and in mystic hymns men delighted to term it "the heart of the world" ($\kappa\alpha\rho\delta\acute{\iota}\alpha$ $\tau o\tilde{\upsilon}$ $\kappa\acute{o}\sigma\mu o\upsilon$).

Thus the bright star of day, set in the midst of the celestial spheres, by the power of its heat vivifies the immense macrocosm through which its fires radiate. Henceforth it will no longer be celebrated, in verse and in prose, merely as the power which, besides light, brings to the world below warmth, fertility, and joy; the ancient conception is amplified and rendered more precise by the touch of science: the sun will become the conductor of the cosmic harmony, the master of the four elements and the four seasons, the heavenly power which, by the invariable changes of its annual course, produces, nourishes, and destroys animals and plants, and by the alternation of day and night warms and cools, dries or moistens the earth and the atmosphere. But, above all, in sidereal religion it will be that supreme regulator of the movements of the stars which at every moment inspires their ever-changing motions, that to which they owe all their qualities and perhaps even (as some believed) their light. Pliny already recognised it as the sovereign divinity which governed nature, *principale naturae regimen ac numen.*[1]

But this universe, so well ordered, cannot be driven by a blind force. The sun, which directs the harmonious movements of the cosmic organism, will, then, be a fire endowed with reason, an intelligent light (φῶς νοερόν). It will be regarded by heathen theologians as the reason which controls the world, *mens mundi et temperatio.*[2] The most important corollaries will be drawn from this, for the sun, the reason of the world, will become the creator of the particular reason which directs the human microcosm. To it is attributed the formation of souls. Its glowing disk, darting its rays upon the earth, constantly sent particles of fire into the bodies which it called to life, and after death, as we shall see,[3] it caused them to reascend to it. Such, in its broad outlines, is the scientific theology which provided both a foundation and a justification for Roman Sun-worship.

From astronomical speculations the Chaldeans had deduced a whole system of religious dogmas. The sun, set in the midst of the superimposed planets, regulates their harmonious movements. As its heat impels them forward, then draws them back, it is constantly influencing, according to its various aspects, the direction of their course and their action upon the earth. Fiery heart of the world, it vivifies the whole of this great organism, and as the stars obey its commands, it reigns supreme

---

[1] Plin., *Nat. Hist.*, ii, 5, § 13.
[2] Cic., *Somn. Scip.*, 4.
[3] See below, Lecture VI, p. 103.

over the universe. The radiance of its splendour illumines the divine immensity of the heavens, but at the same time in its brilliance there is intelligence; it is the origin of all reason, and, as a tireless sower, it scatters unceasingly on the world below the seeds of a harvest of souls. Our brief life is but a particular form of the universal life. Physical theories, applied to the movements of the planets to and fro, will be extended to the relations of the King of the stars with the psychic essences which are subject to him. By a succession of emissions and absorptions he will alternately cause these fiery emanations to descend into the bodies which they animate, and after death will gather them up and make them reascend into his bosom. This coherent and magnificent theology, founded upon the discoveries of ancient astronomy in its zenith, gradually imposed on mankind the cult of the "Invincible Sun" as the master of all nature, creator and preserver of men.

This Sun-worship was the final form which Roman paganism assumed. In 274 the emperor Aurelian, as we have seen,[1] conferred on it official recognition when, on his return from Syria, inspired by what he had seen at Palmyra, he founded a gorgeous temple in honour of *Sol invictus*, served by priests who had precedence even over the members of the ancient *Collegium pontificum*; and in the following century, the Claudian emperors worshipped the almighty star not only as the patron but also as the author of its race. The invincible Sun, raised to the supreme position in the divine hierarchy, peculiar protector of sovereigns and of the Empire, tends to absorb or subordinate to himself all the other divinities of ancient Olympus.

These Emperors thus recognised the superiority over Roman idolatry of this cosmic religion of the East, which the speculations of theologians had elevated to a kind of monotheism. A still closer approach to the Christian conception was obtained. This astronomic pantheism, which deified the world, having the Sun for its centre, readily agreed with Stoic hylozoism. Without much difficulty it was harmonised with the ancient theory which placed the seat of divinity in the highest sphere, that of the fixed stars; but from the time of its expansion it was

[1] See above, Lecture IV, p. 55.

engaged in a struggle against those who, following Plato and Aristotle, set God outside the limits of all the universe, representing him as a Being no longer immanent, but transcendent, distinct from all matter. Philo the Jew was not the only man to reproach the Chaldeans with worshipping the creation instead of the creator. Oriental cults were bound to make early concessions to this idealism, and from the second century, even among the Syrian priests, the doctrine is found to prevail that a Jupiter "Most High" sits in the ether which spreads above the vault of the highest heaven (*Iupiter summus exsuperantissimus*). The Sun henceforth becomes a subordinate power, a reflexion or sensible expression of a superior divinity. But in order to avoid breaking with tradition, from the luminary which gives us light was detached that universal "Reason," of which the Sun had hitherto been the focus, and the existence of another purely spiritual sun was postulated, which shone and reigned in the world of intelligence (νοερὸς κόσμος), and to this were transferred the qualities which henceforth appeared incompatible with matter. We can follow this doctrinal evolution in the works of the Neo-Platonists, and discern its termination in the speculations of Julian the Apostate. The "intelligent" Sun (νοερός) becomes the intermediary between the "intelligible" God (νοητός) and the visible universe.

≈   ≈

We have rapidly sketched the system of theology which was imposed on the Empire. Let us in conclusion attempt to set before ourselves what a revolution these ideas produced in paganism. At the moment when they expanded over the Latin world, the mass of the people still remained almost entirely in the ancient state of idolatry which was contemporary with the Punic wars, and the rustic superstitions of the peasants of Latium still found expression in the pontifical ritual of the Roman people. The learned theology which spread from the East, elevated and enlarged religious thought by holding out an infinitely more lofty conception of divinity. This pantheism stoutly asserted the unity of the world, governed by a supreme intelligence, but in this vast organism, all the parts of which acted and reacted upon each other, man, a privileged creature, was connected with the sidereal gods by a close relationship. His eye perceived their distant light. His divine reason in virtue of its nature could grasp divine truths. In place of the inhabitants of Olympus a kind of supermen, born in time and exempted only from old age and death, it conceived everlasting beings, unwearied and invincible, who ceaselessly ran their changeless course throughout an endless series of ages; in place of gods bound to a city or to a country and, so to speak, *adscripti glebae*, differing with the diversity of peoples, it reverenced universal—or, as they were already called, "catholic"—powers, whose activity, regulated by the revolutions of the celestial spheres, extended over all the earth and embraced the whole human race. An almost anarchical society of Immortals, whose feeble and capricious will raised doubts as to their power, was replaced by the idea of a harmonious *ensemble* of sidereal gods, who, irresistibly guided by the Sun, the heart of the world, the source of all movement and all intelligence, imposed everywhere the inevitable laws of omnipotent Destiny, —last but not least in place of the old methods of divination, now fallen into discredit, of deceitful portents and ambiguous oracles, astrology promised to substitute a scientific method, founded on an experience of almost infinite duration; astrology claimed the power of deciphering with certainty the hitherto inscrutable book of the sky, and of determining the destiny of individuals with the same precision as the date of an eclipse.

We can understand how the amplitude of this masterly conception would raise men's enthusiasm and inspire poets, how it would appear like a complete revelation of the world, and how, in combination at first with Stoic philosophy, then modified by Platonic idealism, the ancient "Chaldean" creed should have been able so long to resist Christianity, the triumph of which it had nevertheless prepared.

The same Semitic race which brought about the fall of paganism is also that which put forth the most powerful effort to save it.

LECTURE V. *Astral Mysticism*[1]*—Ethics and Cult*

A theology which was based on theories of celestial mechanism, which deified mere abstractions such as Time and its subdivisions, which attributed a sacred character to numbers themselves, must, it would seem, have been repellent by reason of its dry metaphysical character. A creation of astronomers, it would appear to have been incapable of appealing to any but an intellectual *élite*, and of winning over any but speculative minds. We might well be astonished, at first sight, that a religion so arid and abstruse should have been able to conquer the ancient world, and we ask ourselves how it obtained a hold over men's souls and was able to attract a multitude of believers.

The answer is that this potent system, which set itself to satisfy the intelligence, made a yet more effective appeal to emotion. If the cults of the East pretended to answer all the questions which man asks concerning the world and himself, they also aimed at stirring his emotions, at arousing in him the rapture of ecstasy.

The leaning towards mysticism, which is one of the characteristic traits of the Syrian Posidonius, was shared by all the adepts of "Chaldean" creeds. We must attempt to analyse here the character of this sidereal mysticism, an original form of devotion, if there ever was one, a curious and little known expression of religious feeling in the days of antiquity, and to show what system of ethics sprang from it, what form of worship corresponded to it, and how it was reconciled with fatalism. After the theory, we pass on to the practice.

[1] See my paper, *Le mysticisme astral dans l'antiquité* (Bulletins de l'Acad. royale de Belgique), Mai, 1909.

The magnificent appearance of the glittering sky has always vividly impressed mankind, and whoever has enjoyed the soft brilliance of an Eastern night, will understand how in that country adoration was naturally excited for the inextinguishable centres of light on high. But this "cosmic emotion," as it has been termed, varies constantly according to the idea which has been formed of the universe. There is assuredly an enormous distance between the views of primitive man, who, when he raised his eyes to the firmament, sometimes dreaded lest this solid vault should fall and crush him, and the veneration of a Kant, who, when considering the stellar systems piled up to infinity above him, felt himself seized with the same respectful wonder that he bestowed on the moral law which he apprehended within him by reason. The feeling has been developed with the progress of knowledge, and in proportion to the precision to which ideas of immensity and eternity attained. In the Greeks the *cosmos* did not arouse, as in ourselves, the troublesome thought of an extension prolonged to infinity beyond the most distant nebulæ which the telescope can reach. The world then had limits. Above the sphere of the fixed stars, which surrounded it on all sides, the ancients supposed that there was nothing but a void or ether. Heaven in their astronomy was like the earth in their geography, a much more limited expression than it is nowadays. The vastness of the visible constellations was not so overwhelming to them as it is to our scientific knowledge, and the distances at which they fixed these bodies, did not suggest to them as to us a distance so great that its extent transcends the limits of our imagination and even figures cannot enable us to realise it. When they gazed into the depths of space, they were not seized to the same degree as we with giddiness at the abysses, nor crushed by the feeling of their own littleness. They would not have cried like Pascal, when meditating on the disproportion between man and nature, incommensurable and speechless: "The eternal silence of these boundless spaces frightens me." [1] The feeling which struck the ancients was mainly one of admiration. Seneca [2]

---

[1] "Le silence éternel de ces espaces infinis m'effraie." (Pascal, *Pensées*.)
[2] Seneca, *De Beneficiis*, iv, 23.

develops this thought, that the stars, even if we do not bear in mind the benefits which they diffuse over our earthly abode, provoke our wonder by their beauty and demand our veneration by their majesty.

From the passages which are devoted to celebrating their splendour, I will quote only one, the final touch of which will make clear the entire difference which separates the ancient from the modern conception. Manilius ends his fifth book by a grandiose description of the brilliance of those moonless nights when even stars of the sixth magnitude kindle their crowded and gleaming fires, seeds of light amid the darkness. The glittering temples of the sky then shine with torches more numerous than the sands of the seashore, than the flowers of the meadow, than the waves of the ocean, than the leaves of the forest. "If nature," adds the poet, "had given to this multitude powers in proportion to its numbers, the ether itself would not have been able to support its own flames, and the conflagration of Olympus would have consumed the entire world."[1]

We have seen[2] how admiration for the beauty of the cosmos, the discovery of the celestial harmony, had led to the declaration of the existence of a guiding Providence. But this is not the most characteristic side of the doctrine: all systems of theology invoke the order of nature as a proof of the existence of God. What is more original is that they took this "cosmic emotion" which every man feels and transformed it into a religious sentiment.

The resplendent stars, which eternally pursue their silent course above us, are divinities endowed with personality and animated by feelings. On the other hand, the soul is a particle detached from the cosmic fires. The warmth which animates the human microcosm, is part of the same substance which vivifies the universe, the reason which guides us partakes of the nature of those luminaries which enlighten it.[3] Itself a fiery

---

[1] Manil., v, 742:

> Cui si pro numero vires natura dedisset,
> Ipse suas aether flammas sufferre nequiret,
> Totus et accenso mundus flagraret Olympo.

[2] See above, Lecture IV, p. 57.

[3] See above, Lectures I, p. 20; II, p. 40; IV, p. 73.

essence, it is kin to the gods which glitter in the firmament. Thus contemplation of the heaven becomes a communion. The desire which man feels to fix his eyes long upon the star-spangled vault, is a divine passion which transports him. A call from heaven draws him towards the radiant spaces. In the splendour of the night his spirit is intoxicated with the glow which the fires above shed upon him. As men possessed, or as the corybantes in the delirium of their orgies, he gives himself up to ecstasy, which frees him from the trammels of his flesh and lifts him, far above the mists of our atmosphere, into the serene regions where move the everlasting stars. Borne on the wings of enthusiasm, he projects himself into the midst of this sacred choir and follows its harmonious movements. Then he partakes in the life of these luminous gods, which from below he sees twinkling in the radiance of the ether; before the appointed hour of death he participates in their divinity, and receives their revelations in a stream of light, which by its brilliance dazzles even the eye of reason.

Such are the sublime effusions in which the mystic eloquence of a Posidonius delights. Nevertheless in this learned theology, whose first authors were astronomers, erudition never loses its rights. Man, attracted by the brightness of the sky, does not only take an unspeakable delight in considering the rhythmic dance of the stars, regulated by the harmonies of a divine music produced by the movements of the celestial spheres. Never weary of this ever-repeated spectacle, he does not confine himself to enjoying it. The thirst for knowledge, which is innate in him, impels him to enquire what is the nature of these glowing bodies whose radiance reaches him, to discover the causes and the laws of their unceasing movements. He aspires to compre-hend the course of the constellations and the sinuous path of the planets, which should reveal to him the rules of life and the secrets of destiny. As soon as he approaches the limits of the heavens, his desire to understand them is inflamed by the actual facility which he experiences in satisfying it. The transports which draw him towards the higher regions, do not dull but enlighten his mind. Are not all discoveries of astronomy revelations of their nature made by the sidereal gods to their earnest disciples? This mystic contemplation of heaven, source of all intelligence, will be the religious ideal of lofty spirits. The astronomer Ptolemy, who of all the savants of antiquity had perhaps the most influence on succeeding generations, will forget his complicated calculations and his arduous researches to sing of this intoxication. We have preserved the following lines of his [1]: "Mortal as I am, I know that I am born for a day, but when I follow the serried multitude of the stars in their circular course, my feet no longer touch the earth; I ascend to Zeus himself to feast me on ambrosia, the food of the gods."

Let us compare this serene ecstasy with the transports of Dionysiac intoxication, such as Euripides for example depicts for us so strikingly in the Bacchæ, and we shall at once realise the distance which separates this astral religion from the earlier paganism. In the one, under the stimulus of wine, the soul communicates with the exuberant forces of nature, and the overflowing energy of physical life expresses itself in tumultuous exaltation of the senses and impetuous disorder of the spirit. In the other, it is with pure light that reason quenches her thirst for truth; and "the abstemious intoxication," [2] which exalts her to the stars, kindles in her no ardour save a passionate yearning for divine knowledge. The source of mysticism is transferred from earth to heaven.

We, who in our northern towns scarcely perceive the light of the stars, continually veiled in fogs and dimmed by smoke, we to whom they are merely bodies in a state of incandescence moved by mechanical forces, we can hardly comprehend the strength of the religious feeling which they inspired in the men of old. The indefinable impression which is produced by the great spectacles of nature, the desire which possesses us of probing the causes of her phenomena, were in their case combined with the aspirations of faith towards these "visible gods," who were ever present to be worshipped. The passion for knowledge, the ardour of devotion, were blended in the deep emotion which was stirred by the idea of a communion between man and the harmony of the skies.

[1] *Anthol. Palat.*, ix, 577.
[2] *Νηφάλιος μέθη* (Philo).

Think of the prestige which such a theory gave to the astrologer who is in constant relation with the divine stars. It is nowhere more clearly expressed than in a passage of a rhetorician belonging to the Augustan age, Arellius Fuscus.[1] "He to whom the gods themselves reveal the future, who imposes their will even on kings and peoples, cannot be fashioned," he says, "by the same womb which bore us ignorant men. His is a superhuman rank. Confidant of the gods, he is himself divine." Then he adds:

If the pretensions of astrology are genuine, why do not men of every age devote themselves to this study? Why from our infancy do we not fix our eyes on nature and on the gods, seeing that the stars unveil themselves for us, and that we can live in the midst of the gods? Why exhaust ourselves in efforts to acquire eloquence, or devote ourselves to the profession of arms? Rather let us lift up our minds by means of the science which reveals to us the future, and before the appointed hour of death let us taste the pleasures of the Blest.

This lofty conception, which was formed of astrology, queen of sciences, this mysticism which gave it a sacred character, entailed ethical consequences of extreme importance. The *mathematici* of the Roman empire were the successors of the ancient Chaldean priests, and they never forgot it. They love to assume the holy guise of incorruptible prophets, and to consider the exercise of their profession as a priesthood. They are fond of laying stress on the purity of their morals, and they complacently enumerate all the qualities which bring them near to the divine nature,—chastity, sobriety, integrity, self-renunciation. If others seek fortune at the price of a thousand efforts, the astrologer, dedicated to arduous research, is bound to surrender himself entirely to be penetrated by the intelligence of God.

"Impendendus homo est, deus esse ut possit in ipso."[2]

---

[1] Seneca., *Suasor.*, 4.
[2] Manilius, iv, 407.

Thus astrologers, who profess to discover the mysteries of fate, lead an austere life, or at any rate they affect it. This is the very condition of their power. Mortals do not share in the heavenly ecstasy, unless they have merited it by the morality of their conduct. Science is a revelation promised to virtue. Man must be purified from all defilement in order to render himself worthy of the society of the gods, and of the knowledge of heavenly things. This idea, that a man's vices weigh him down and detain him here below, is frequently found developed. The doctrine contrasts the body formed of earth with the sacred fire of the spirit. All carnal desires in some measure materialise this sacred fire at the same time that they pollute it, and hinder it from ascending to the ether. On the other hand, if the soul emancipates itself from the passions of the body, it will be able to fly lightly and easily to the stars. In the vehement polemic which Posidonius launches against Epicurus, he reproaches him,[1] in regard to his astronomical doctrines, with having been "blinder than a mole," and he adds: "No wonder, for to discover the real nature of things is not the part of men devoted to pleasure, but of those whose virtuous character makes the good their ideal, and who do not prefer to it the comfort of their beloved flesh." The absurdity of the cosmography professed by the Epicureans is, in his eyes, a consequence of their dissolute life. Here we see set forth the idea, so dangerously developed later, that true knowledge is the reward of piety.

The marvels of nature produce on us a mysterious impression. The view of immensity elevates us above the vulgarities of life. This feeling, innate in man, astral religion has seized upon and developed splendidly in order to make it a source of morality. Theologians celebrate the spiritual joys which this religion has in store for its adepts, the intensity of which renders all material delights insipid and contemptible; in a hundred ways they contrast the meanness of earthly with the splendour of heavenly things. How should the worshippers of the sky take delight in chariot-races, or be seduced by the songs and dances of the theatre, they who have the privilege of contemplating the gods

[1] Cleomedes, *De Motu Circul.*, ii, 1, § 87.

and of listening to their prophetic voices? How utterly do their thoughts, which move among the stars, scorn from the heights of this resplendent abode the gilded palaces and the pompous luxury of wealth! They heap not up silver and gold, treasures worthy of the dark places of the earth from which avarice draws them, but they fill their souls with spiritual riches and make them masters of all nature, in such wise that their possessions extend to the confines of the East and of the West. Even the privations of exile cannot touch them, since under all climes they find the same stars at the same distance from their watchful eyes. Can they but mingle with them, and their souls mount to the bright regions to which they are drawn by their kinship with the heavenly fires, it matters but little to them what earth they tread with their feet. Absorbed in her sublime researches, our reason will disdain the perishable goods of this life and the gross pleasures of the multitude. She will free herself from all the carnal desires aroused in her by the body, fashioned of earth. Thus devotion to science is surrounded in sidereal worship with a halo of religion. The exaltation of intellectual life, which alone is divine, leads here to asceticism.

🖐   🖐

Astral mysticism, we see, conceived a blissful state of mind where man, even on earth, freed himself of all that was earthly, emancipated himself from the needs of the body, as from bonds, and from the impulses born of it, to devote himself to the contemplation of nature and of the starry sky, which imparted to him direct knowledge of divine activity. This ideal, sternly ascetic, in that it set the satisfaction of bodily instincts in sharp opposition to the aspirations of sovereign reason, led to a life of self-renunciation, illumined only by the sacred joys of study. But has man's will the power to choose this happy lot? Does not astrology formulate a principle destructive of all morality and all religion, the principle of fatalism?

Fatalism indeed is the capital principle which astrology imposed on the world. The Chaldeans were the first to conceive the idea of Necessity dominating the universe.[1] This is

---

[1] See above, Lecture I, p. 17.

also one of the ruling ideas of the Stoics.[1] An absolute determinism is implied in all the postulates of the science of stellar influence on human life, and Manilius has expressed it in a striking line:

"Fata regunt orbem, certa stant omnia lege."[2]

The power of this fatalistic conception in ancient times may be estimated by its long-continued survival, at least in the East, where it originated. From the Alexandrine period, it spread over the whole Hellenic world, and at the close of paganism it is still against this doctrine that the efforts of Christian apologetics are mainly directed, but it was destined to outlast all attacks and even to impose itself on Islam. For, Mahommedanism is, in this respect, the heir of paganism.

The capital objection which its adversaries, whether heathen or Christian, never ceased to advance against it,—the dialectic of Carneades made already brilliant use of this weapon,—is the same that the defenders of the doctrine of free will have never ceased to repeat—namely, that the absence of free will destroys responsibility: rewards and punishments are meaningless if men act under a dominating necessity; if they are born heroes or criminals, morality entails no merit and immorality no reproach. We cannot set forth here the metaphysical discussions provoked by this controversy, which always has been, and always will be, carried on. But, from a practical point of view, Stoicism proved by facts—an irrefutable argument in ethics— that fatalism is not incompatible with a manly and active virtue. Nay more, it was possible to regard it as giving a religious basis to virtue, if virtue resulted from the accord of microcosm and macrocosm which found its highest expression in ecstasy. Some modern thinkers, like Schleiermacher, have made true religion consist in the feeling, on the part of the creature, of absolute dependence on the infinite Cause of the universe. Astrology, by strengthening this feeling of dependence, has been a source of real piety. Its professors elevate to a duty complete resignation to omnipotent fate, cheerful acceptance

[1] See above, Lecture II, p. 40.
[2] Manil., iv, 14.

of the inevitable. They declare themselves submissive to destiny even the most capricious, like an intelligent slave who guesses his master's wishes in order to satisfy them, and can make the harshest servitude tolerable. This passionate surrender, this eagerness to submit to divine Fate inspired certain souls in days of old with feelings so fervent as to recall the rapture of Christian devotion, which burns to subject itself to the will of God. It has been observed that the renunciation of Demetrius, quoted by Seneca,[1] affords a singular parallel to one of the most famous Christian prayers, the "Suscipe" of St. Ignatius, which ends the book of *Spiritual Exercises*:

I have but one complaint to address to you, immortal gods, that you did not make me sooner know your will. I would myself have anticipated what, at your call, I offer to submit to now. Would you take my children? It is for you that I have reared them. Do you desire some part of my body? Take it from me; it is but a slight sacrifice I make, since I must soon leave it altogether. Do you desire my life? Why should I hesitate to restore to you that which you gave me? . . . I am not constrained to aught, I suffer nought against my will, I am not obedient to God, I am in accord with him, and the more so, because I know that everything takes place in virtue of an immutable law proclaimed from all eternity.

It is the ideal of pure Stoicism that is expressed in this effusion, but, if it cannot be called anti-religious, it was at least in contradiction to all established religions. If an irrevocable Destiny is imposed on us, no sacred ceremony can change its decrees. Worship is unavailing, it is idle to demand from divination the secrets of a future which nothing can alter, and prayers—to use an expression of Seneca[2]—are nothing but the consolations of sickly souls.

And without doubt certain spirits, as Suetonius states of the Emperor Tiberius,[3] "fully convinced that everything is ruled by Fate, neglected the practice of religion." The astrologer Vettius Valens[4] declares it useless. "It is impossible to defeat

[1] Seneca, *De Provid.*, v, 5.
[2] Seneca, *Quæst. Nat.*, ii, 35, "*Aegrae mentis solacia.*"
[3] Suetonius, *Vita Tib.*, 69.
[4] Vettius Valens, v, 9 (p. 220, 28 ed, Kroll).

by sacrifice that which has been established from the beginning of time." We must therefore reverence the superior power which rules the universe, without demanding aught of it, and we must content ourselves with the joy which is caused by a feeling of intimate union of creature with creator.

But ordinary people did not rise to this haughty ideal of piety. A Peripatetic of the third century, Alexander of Aphrodisias, has forcibly characterised the want of logic which led the majority of mankind to act in contradiction to their theories. [1]

Those [he says] who maintain energetically in their discourses that Fate is inevitable and who attribute all events to it, seem to place no reliance on it in the actions of their own lives. For they call upon Fortune, thus recognising that it has an action independent of Fate; and moreover they never cease to pray to the gods, as though these could grant their prayers even in opposition to Fate; and they do not hesitate to have recourse to omens, as though it were possible for them, by learning any fated event in advance, to guard themselves against it. The reasons which they invent to establish a harmony between their theories and their conduct, are but pitiful sophisms.

And in fact, as a Christian writer of the fourth century observes, if the pagans of Rome were about to marry, if they intended to make a purchase, or aspired to some dignity, they hastened to ask the soothsayer for prognostications, while at the same time praying the Fates to grant them years of prosperity.

A fundamental inconsistency which we noted from the beginning [2] is obvious in all this development of astrology, which professed to become an exact science, but which always remained a sacerdotal theology. The stars were regarded as divine at Babylon before the doctrine of universal determinism had been constructed, and this character was preserved—in defiance of logic. In the temples of Oriental gods astrology assumed, or rather maintained, a very different character from that under which it presented itself in the schools or the observatories. A didactic treatise like the *Tetrabiblos* of Ptolemy,

[1] Alex. Aphrod., *De Anima Mantissa*, p. 182, 18 ed. Bruns.
[2] See above, Lecture I., p. 18.

where the effects of the planets are traced to physical causes, could never have become the gospel of any sect. In the sidereal cults Fortune will no longer be represented as a goddess blind and deaf, who with unreasoning favour or implacable malignity makes sport of deserving and undeserving alike. Less stress will be laid on the all-powerfulness of Necessity than upon the divinity of the stars. These were no longer merely cosmic forces, whose propitious or unpropitious operation was weakened or strengthened according to the windings of a course fixed from all eternity. The old mythology had not here been reduced to mathematical formulæ. The celestial bodies had remained gods and goddesses, endowed with senses and qualities, sometimes wroth but always placable, who could be propitiated by prayers and offerings. Occult ceremonies, magical incantations, had, it was thought, the power of rescuing even here below the faithful from the enslavement which Destiny caused to lie heavy on the rest of mankind, nay more, of bending the celestial spirits to the will of the believer. Even the theorist Firmicus Maternus, though vigorously asserting the omnipotence of Fate, invokes the aid of the gods to enable him to resist the influence of the stars.

Sidereal determinism, pushed to its extreme consequences, was a theory of despair, the weight of which crushed the man. He felt himself mastered, overpowered by blind forces which impelled him as irresistibly as they caused the celestial spheres to move. His mind sought to escape from the oppression of this cosmic mechanism, to free itself from the slavery in which 'Aνάγκη held it. No longer was reliance placed upon the ceremonies of ancient cults to rescue him from the rigour of her dominion, but Oriental religions provided the remedy for the evil which they had spread. The new master who has possessed himself of the sky will be propitiated by new means. Not only magic but also mysteries profess to teach methods for exorcising Fate. They will be able to appease the wrath of sidereal powers, and to win their favour by rites and offerings; they will teach above all how to prolong man's life beyond the term appointed by Destiny, and to assure him an immortality of bliss.[1]

[1] See below, Lecture VI, p. 100 ss.

Thus belief in Fate not only (1) became a source of moral inspiration to noble minds, but also (2) provided a justification of the necessity of positive worship.

Concerning the worship which was paid to the stars in the West we possess very few data, even for the most important of all, that of the Sun. I will not lay stress on certain details which have come down to us about the rites of the Moon, the stars, the signs of the zodiac, etc. We shall only mention some liturgical practices which have had permanent results.

It was customary to worship the rising Sun (*Oriens*) at dawn, at the moment when its first rays struck the demons who invaded the earth in the darkness. Tacitus describes to us how, at the battle of Bedriacum in A.D. 69, the soldiers of Vespasian saluted the rising sun with loud shouts after the Syrian custom. [1] In temples thrice a day—at dawn, at midday, and at dusk—a prayer was addressed to the heavenly source of light, the worshipper turning towards the East in the morning, towards the South at midday, and towards the West in the evening. Perhaps this custom survived in the three daily services of the early Church.

A very general observance required that on the 25th of December the birth of the "new Sun" should be celebrated, when after the winter solstice the days began to lengthen and the "invincible" star triumphed again over darkness. It is certain that the date of this *Natalis Invicti* was selected by the Church as the commemoration of the *Nativity* of Jesus, which was previously confused with the Epiphany. In appointing this day, universally marked by pious rejoicings, which were as far as possible retained,—for instance the old chariot-races were preserved,—the ecclesiastical authorities purified in some degree the customs which they could not abolish. This substitution, which took place at Rome probably between 354 and 360, was adopted throughout the Empire, and that is why we still celebrate Christmas on the 25th of December.

The pre-eminence assigned to the *dies Solis* also certainly

[1] Tacit., *Hist.*, iii, 24.

contributed to the general recognition of Sunday as a holiday. This is connected with a more important fact, namely, the adoption of the week by all European nations. We have seen that in the astrological system each day was sacred to a planet. It is probable that the worshipper prayed to the presiding star of each day in turn. We still possess the text of these prayers addressed to the planets in the East as in the West. We have some in Greek, but of a late date, and the most curious are those of the pagans of Harran near Edessa, which an Arabic writer has transmitted to us in great detail. Thus, for instance, to call upon Saturn it was necessary to await the favourable moment, to don black vestments, to approach the sacred place humbly, like a man sunk in sorrow, to burn a perfume composed of incense and opium mixed with grease and the urine of a goat, then, at the moment when the smoke arose, to raise the eyes to the star and say:

"Lord, whose name is august, whose power is widespread, whose spirit sublime, O Lord Saturn the cold, the dry, the dark, the harmful, . . . crafty sire who knowest all wiles, who art deceitful, sage, understanding, who causest prosperity or ruin, happy or unhappy is he whom thou makest such. I adjure thee, O primeval Father, by thy great mercies, and thy noble qualities, to do for me this and that!"

"This having been said," continues the text, which I am abridging, "thou shalt bow thyself down with humility and contrition, and while bending thou shalt repeat the prayer several times."

We do not suppose that in the Roman Empire devotees would have gone through such complicated ceremonies every day in honour of the planets,—the great prayer to Jupiter fills not less than four pages,—but certainly the use of an analogous liturgy in certain cults, notably in the mysteries of Mithra, contributed largely to the adoption of the week throughout the Roman Empire.

This diffusion of the week and even its invention are much more recent than is usually supposed. It is known that the Jews already divided time into consecutive groups of seven days ending with the Sabbath, but these days were not each under the patronage of a planet: they were merely counted. This system of the measurement of time originates in the division of the lunar month into four equal parts. This hebdomadal period is also found elsewhere, but the astrological *week* has a much later origin. It is connected with the general theory of "chronocratories," which assigned to each planet the dominion over an hour, a day, a year, and even over a period of a thousand years [1]; and the assignment of each of these to one of the gods is the result of an ingenious calculation, which is based on the so-called "Chaldean" arrangement of the planets. Now this arrangement appears nowhere before the second century B.C., and it may be considered certain that our week is a creation of the Hellenistic period. It was probably first introduced into the sidereal cults of Mesopotamia and of Syria, thence passed to Alexandria, and it is about the age of Augustus that it began to supplant in Latin countries the old Roman *nundinum* of eight days, and it ended by replacing all local calendars. Adopted by the Church, in spite of its suspicious origin, it was imposed on all Christian peoples. When to-day we name the days Saturday, Sunday, Monday, we are heathen and astrologers without knowing it, since we recognise implicitly that the first belongs to Saturn, the second to the Sun, and the third to the Moon.

If I may be allowed to conclude with an observation, which takes us a little away from our subject, there can perhaps be no more striking proof of the power and popularity of astrological beliefs than the influence which they have exercised over popular language. All modern idioms preserve traces of it, which we can no longer discern save with difficulty, survivals of vanished superstitions. Do we still remember, when we speak of a martial, jovial, or lunatic character, that it must have been formed by Mars, Jupiter, or the Moon, that an *influence* is the effect of a fluid emitted by the celestial bodies, that it is one of these "*astra*" which, if hostile, will cause me a *disaster*, and that, finally, if I have the good fortune to find myself among you, I certainly owe it to my *lucky star*?

[1] See above, Lecture IV, p. 67.

LECTURE VI. *Eschatology*

In the previous lecture we showed how, to the astronomer theologians, contemplation of the sky had become the source of a mystic union with the divine stars. The sublime joys of ecstasy, which brings man into communion with the sidereal gods, give him but a foretaste of the bliss which is in store for him when after death his soul, ascending to the celestial spheres, shall penetrate all their mysteries. The transient exaltation, which illumines his intelligence here below, is a dim foreshadowing of the intoxication which will be wrought in him by the immediate prospect of the stars and the full comprehension of truth. The most ideal pursuits of the sage in this world are but a faint adumbration of a blessedness which will be perfected in the life to come.

Thus astral mysticism based upon a psychological experience the construction of a complete doctrine of immortality. It glorified its ideal of earthly life and projected it into the life beyond. These ideas, as they spread throughout the Roman world, could not fail to modify profoundly the whole conception of man's destiny. In to-day's lecture we shall devote ourselves to exhibiting this transformation.

At the beginning of the Empire the ancient beliefs concerning existence beyond the grave, the idea that the dead man lived a gloomy life in the tomb, sustained by the funeral offerings of his descendants, retained hardly any influence, and the mythological tales about the Styx, Charon's barque, and the punishments inflicted in the nether world no longer obtained any credence. Philosophical criticism had shown the absurdity of these lugubrious chimeras. Greek philosophy in general aimed at realising the *summum bonum* in this world. Of the two great systems which were predominant at Rome, one flatly denied a future life. It is well known that Epicurus taught that the soul is composed of atoms and is dissolved with the body, and there is no doctrine of the Master on which his disciples insist with more complacent assurance. Lucretius[1] praises him for having driven from men's minds "this dread of Acheron which troubles the life of man to its inmost depths." The other great philosophical school, Stoicism, showed considerable hesitation concerning the fate in store for our souls. Its various representatives held different views on this point. Panætius, the friend of the Scipios, one of the writers who contributed most to win Rome over to the tenets of the Porch, resolutely declined to believe in a survival of the individual. In reality it is in this world that true Stoicism places the realisation of its ideal. For it the aim of existence is not the preparation for death but the attainment of perfect virtue. By giving freedom from the passions, virtue confers independence and felicity. The sage, a happy being, is a god on earth, and heaven can offer nothing more to him. In this system eschatological theories had only a secondary importance, and that explains their variations.

The negative point of view adopted by Panætius is that of the majority, perhaps, of the theorists of astrology. Among those who prided themselves on philosophy, many denied immortality or at least doubted it, as for instance Ptolemy, who was influenced by the ideas of the Peripatetics, or Vettius Valens, who represents purer Stoicism. According to them the divine spark which animated bodies, became merged after death in the cosmic fires, from which it had issued, without preserving any individuality. From death, then, they expected nothing but liberation from Destiny, of which they were the bondsmen here below; henceforth they were freed from those cruel necessities and pitiless vicissitudes to which those beings are subject who live under the planetary vaults. Their conception of existence and their highest aspirations were those to which the most antique of modern poets has given forcible

[1] Lucret., III, 37:

Et metus, ille foras praeceps Acheruntis agendus
Funditus humanam qui vitam turbat ab imo.

expression; I mean Leconte de Lisle, who, adopting a defini-
tion of Alfred de Vigny, declared that life is "a sombre incident
between two endless periods of sleep." His musical and des-
pondent apostrophe is well known [1]:

"Et toi, divine Mort, où tout rentre et s'efface,
    Accueille tes enfants dans ton sein étoilé,
    Affranchis nous du temps, du nombre, et de l'espace,
    Et rends nous le repose que la vie a troublé." [2]

This pessimism, which regarded annihilation as a blessing,
might be accepted by certain spirits and sometimes preached
with a kind of passion, as by Pliny in a famous confession of
faith. [3] But the majority, without venturing to admit the
certainty of a future life, clung to it as a comfortable hypothesis
entertained by certain thinkers.

We find it hard to resign ourselves to complete annihilation;
even when reason acquiesces in the destruction of our transitory
being, subconsciously we protest against it. The deep instinct
of self-preservation drives man to desire a continuance of life,
and feeling revolts against the anguish of an irrevocable
separation, against the final loss of all one loves. Moreover in
imperial Rome there were so many unpunished crimes, so
much undeserved suffering, that men naturally took refuge in
the hope of a happier future which would repair all the in-
justices of a sorrowful present. This is the explanation of the
ever-increasing triumph of new theories concerning a life to
come. To the scepticism and the negative views which were
prevalent at the end of the Republic, at least in intellectual
circles, were opposed doctrines taught by the professors of the
theology which found in Posidonius its most illustrious ex-
ponent. A Stoic, he combines the teaching of the Porch with

---

[1] *Poèmes antiques*, "Dies Irae."
[2] O Death divine, at whose recall
    Returneth all
    To fade in thy embrace,
    Gather thy children to thy bosom starred,
    Free us from time, from number, and from space,
    And give us back the rest that life hath marred.
[3] Pliny, *Nat. Hist.*, vii, 55, § 188.

the idealism of Plato, who held that the soul, being an immaterial essence, must rise to a fairer world. But he welcomes also,
and above all, the religious traditions of the Syrians, of which
he is to be the eloquent propagandist.

All Oriental mysteries profess to reveal to their adepts the
secret of attaining to a blessed immortality. In place of the
shifting and contradictory opinions of philosophers concerning
the fate of man after death, these religions offered a certainty
based on a divine revelation and corroborated by the belief of
countless generations which had clung to it. The despairing
world eagerly welcomed these promises, and philosophy, under-
going a transformation, joined with the ancient beliefs of the
East to give to the Empire a new eschatology.

In point of fact, the different cults conceived blessedness
under very different forms, some of them gross enough. To the
followers of Bacchus or of the Phrygian Sabazius drunkenness
is divine possession. The devotee was to be admitted to the feast
of the gods, there to rejoice with them for ever in a state of
pleasant intoxication. The Alexandrine mysteries of Isis and
Serapis diffused a less material conception of future happiness.
The dead will descend to the nether world in full possession of
his body as well as of his soul, and will enjoy an eternal rapture
in contemplating face to face the ineffable beauty of the gods,
whose equal he has become. But of the various beliefs which
secured adepts in the Roman world, none was to become so
influential as that of sidereal eschatology. This is the purest and
most elevated doctrine which can be put to the credit of ancient
paganism, and it was to establish a firm hold on the Western
mind.

We shall attempt to show how it developed, by whom and
when it was disseminated, and what different forms it assumed
in the Græco-Roman world.

❧   ☙

Certain beliefs which are found, side by side with many
others, among primitive peoples, regard the spirits of the dead
as departing to inhabit the moon or the sun, or even fancy that
their evergrowing host forms the multitude of stars or crowds

the long track of the Milky Way. This very ancient idea received a new significance when philosophers, as far back as Heraclitus, taught that the soul is of the same nature as the ether, which is, as it were, the soul of the universe. Just as the one causes our bodies to move, the other, they said, caused the stars to fly across the spaces of the heavens. At death the body fell to dust and was reunited with the earth, but the glowing breath which had animated it, ascended to the luminous fluid that extended above the clouds, and coalesced with this subtle air, which was the source of all life. The official epitaph on the Athenians who fell at Potidæa in 432 B.C., expresses the conviction that the ether has received into its bosom the souls of these heroes as the earth has received their bodies.[1]

There we have an opinion wide-spread in the fifth century from one end of the Hellenic world to the other. In opposition, then, to the views of the Homeric age and of popular belief, these doctrines taught that the abode of souls was neither the tomb nor the nether realm of Pluto, but the upper zone of the universe. Some, with greater exactitude, made them the companions of the stars, whose divinity philosophers devoted themselves to proving.[2] The two ideas are closely related, for the affinity of gods and men is an eminently Greek idea. Some sects of mystics—Orphic or Pythagorean—taught that the spirits of the dead departed to dwell in the moon, or to shine among the constellations. Thus Aristophanes[3] transforms the Pythagorean poet, Ion of Chios, the friend of Sophocles, into the morning star. In Plato's view souls which have made a good use of their lives return to inhabit the heavenly bodies, which served as their dwelling-place before birth, and there partake of the bliss of a divine existence.

Moreover, the Greeks, as we have seen,[4] had long before told how certain heroes of fable had been transported to heaven in reward for their exploits. Hercules, Perseus and Andromeda, the Dioscuri Castor and Pollux, and many others had thus been

---

[1] *Corp. Inscr. Att.*, i, 442: Αἰθὴρ μὲν ψυχὰς ὑπεδέξατο, σώματα δὲ χθών.
[2] See above, Lecture II, p. 23 sqq.
[3] Aristoph., *Pax*, 831.
[4] See above, Lecture IV, p. 65.

metamorphosed into constellations. "Catasterism" forms the *dénoûment* of a number of mythological stories. Hence it did not appear bold to assign to eminent men of the day the same destiny as to the heroes of the past, and no one saw anything offensive in the supposition that their divine spirits took a place in the sky. The astronomer Conon did not hesitate even to recognise there the lock of hair which queen Berenice had dedicated to Aphrodite, and which became thenceforth a new cluster of stars. All persons, animals, and objects whose image men professed to find in the celestial vault, thus had their legends which connected them with some mythological episode or some historical event.

These doctrines, which in this way gradually spread over classical Greece, were to be taken up and transformed by the Stoics. To the disciples of Zeno the soul of man is a portion of that divine fire in which their pantheistic naturalism saw at once the productive force and the intelligence of the world. Human reason, a particle of this universal reason, was conceived as a breath, a fiery emanation. Now the stars are the most brilliant manifestation of the cosmic fire. The philosophy of the Porch, then, favoured the belief that the soul was united with the heavenly bodies by a special relation, and thus Stoicism was readily reconciled with astrology. It is a remarkable fact that this doctrine was defended, in the second century before our era, notably by Hipparchus, who was not only one of the great astronomers but a convinced adept of astrological theories, and, as we have seen,[1] Pliny applauds him warmly for having proved better than any one else that man is related to the stars and that our souls are "a part of the heaven."

Yet the pure Stoics, as we said above, while fully admitting the continued existence of this divine essence which warms and governs the body, inclined to the belief that after death it was reabsorbed into the universal fire without retaining any individuality. But very early this philosophy was led to make concessions to popular beliefs. Certain of its professors sought to bring the new principles which were formulated in the sphere of physics and psychology into agreement with the mystic ideas

[1] See above, Lecture II, p. 40.

propagated by the religious sects which began to spread from Asia over the Græco-Latin world. Posidonius, let us recall the fact, was the most active agent in bringing about this syncretism between East and West, and his pupil Cicero gives us in the *Dream of Scipio* the earliest statement of this eschatology at Rome: The souls of those who have deserved immortality will not descend to the depths of the earth, they will rise again to the starry spheres. We shall return several times to this remarkable *Dream*.

A number of inscriptions attest the extent to which this belief had spread by the first century before our era. There is an unlimited choice of examples to quote. Thus an epitaph on a girl thirteen years old discovered in the island of Thasos [1] says: "In this tomb lies the body of a young maiden, *anthophoros* (flower-bearer) of Ceres, carried off by the merciless Fates. But her soul by the good-will of the Immortals dwells among the stars and takes its place in the sacred choir of the blest." Here is a Latin epitaph,[2] one among many of the same kind: "My divine soul shall not descend to the shades; heaven and the stars have borne me away; earth holds my body, and this stone an empty name." Epigraphy proves that these ideas of a future life became gradually prevalent. They were more and more generally accepted under the Roman Empire in proportion as Oriental religions acquired more authority, and in the last days of paganism they exerted a preponderating influence.

After this rapid sketch of the historical development of sidereal eschatology, we shall attempt to trace the outlines of the doctrine and to show its varieties.

We shall have to examine four points:

1. Who obtains astral immortality?
2. How does the soul ascend to heaven?
3. Where is the abode of the blest to be found?
4. How is the blessedness that is vouchsafed to them conceived?

1. *Who is it that wins the boon of this sidereal immortality?*

It appears certain that in the East it was at first reserved for

[1] Kaibel, *Epigr. Gr.*, 324.
[2] Buecheler, *Carmina Epigr.*, 611.

those monarchs who, while still on earth, were raised by the reverence of their subjects above their fellow-men and put almost, or altogether, on a level with the heavenly powers. Traces of this primitive conception survived even at Rome. According to a tradition which is echoed by Manilius,[1] Nature first revealed her mysteries to the minds of kings, whose lofty thoughts reach the summit of the heavens. Another doctrine was also taught, that the divine souls of sovereigns come from a higher place than those of other men, that the greater a man's dignity, the greater is the dower he gets from heaven. But, in a general way, the rites employed to ensure immortality to kings by putting them on a level with the gods, were by degrees extended to important members of their *entourage*. This was a sort of privilege, of posthumous nobility, which was conferred on great ministers of state, or which they usurped, long before the common crowd of the dead attained it. Such is the idea to which Cicero gives expression in the *Dream of Scipio*[2]: "To all those who have saved, succoured, or exalted their fatherland, there is assigned a fixed place in heaven, where they will enjoy everlasting bliss, for it is from heaven that they who guide and preserve states have descended, thither to reascend." This is the republican paraphrase of the doctrine of the divinity of kings. But if an ex-consul is thus willing to accord apotheosis to statesmen, philosophers claim it for sages, men of letters for great poets, and artists for creative geniuses. Here the old Greek worship of heroes, combined with belief in "catasterism," comes in to enlarge the narrow conception of monarchy. Hermes Trismegistus[3] taught that there were different kinds of royal souls, for there is a royalty of spirit, a royalty of art, a royalty of science, even a royalty of bodily strength. All exceptional men resemble the gods, and the people were loath to believe that they perished for ever. Some modern writers have shared this sentiment. "That a Shah of Persia or a critic of Milan," said Carducci, who had suffered at the hands of the latter class, "dies irrevocably, I believe, and I congratulate

---

[1] Manil., i, 41.

[2] Cic., *Somn. Scip.*, c. 3.

[3] Herm. Trism. ap. Stobaeum, *Ecl.*, p. 466, Wachsmuth.

myself on the belief. But that Mazzini or that Dante Alighieri is utterly dead, I am entirely unconvinced."

Among those heroes whose merits had opened to them the gates of heaven,—"virtus recludens immeritis mori caelum," as Horace puts it,[1]—the military monarchies of the East placed in the forefront the warriors who had died sword in hand in defence of their country, or rather of their king. This doctrine, which was deep-rooted particularly in Syria, has been preserved, as is well known, in Islam. But, side by side with these valiant soldiers, pious priests also were judged to merit immortality, or rather they adjudged it to themselves. Who could be more worthy to mount to the stars than those who, while yet on earth, lived in their society and in contemplation of them? Then, when Oriental mysteries spread, they all professed to prolong the existence of the initiated beyond the hour of death appointed by Destiny and to exempt them from the fatal law imposed on mankind. Participation in the occult ceremonies of worship becomes an infallible means of securing salvation. The gods welcomed amongst them the faithful who had served them fervently and had purified themselves by the scrupulous performance of rites.

But the demands of a less exclusive morality did not allow happiness beyond the grave to be secured as the reward of sectarian piety. Side by side with devotional observances the practice of more essentially human virtues was demanded. The purity necessary to salvation, which was originally ritual purity, now became spiritual. Though priests doubtless insisted strongly on the fulfilment of religious duties, the more philosophical theologians looked, above all, to the psychological conditions necessary for translation to heaven. We have indicated in dealing with the subject of ecstasy,[2]—and we shall return to it shortly,—how souls made gross by carnal passions were unable to ascend to the abode of the gods of light. For those who have not kept themselves pure throughout their lives, a posthumous purification is indispensable.

---

[1] Horace, *Odes*, iii, 2, 21.
[2] See above, Lecture V, p. 83.

60431

2. This brings us to the second question which we have set before ourselves: *How did souls rise to the stars?*

It may be said that originally they made use of every method of locomotion: they ascended to heaven on foot, on horseback, in carriages, and they even had recourse to aviation. Among the ancient Egyptians the firmament was conceived as being so close to the mountains of the earth that it was possible to climb up to it with the aid of a ladder. Although the stars had been relegated to an infinite distance in space, the ladder still survived in Roman paganism as an amulet and as a symbol. Many people continued to place in tombs a small bronze ladder which recalled the naïve beliefs of distant ages; and in the mysteries of Mithra a ladder of seven steps, made of seven different metals, still symbolised the passage of the soul across the planetary spheres.

Though it had become difficult to reach heaven on foot, it was still possible to get there on horseback,—on the back of a winged horse. Thus the large cameo of Paris called "The Apotheosis of Augustus," represents a prince of his house, Germanicus or Marcellus, borne by a "Pegasus," which doubtless has no connection with Bellerophon's mount. Sometimes a griffin is preferred to Pegasus: the monster flies heavenwards carrying on its sturdy back the deceased raised to the level of the gods. The dead, however, more frequently travelled in a car,—the car of the Sun. The idea that the divine charioteer drives a team across the heavenly fields existed in very early times in Syria as well as in Babylon, Persia, and Greece. The horses of fire and the chariot of fire, which carried up the prophet Elijah in a whirlwind, are very probably the horses and chariot of the Sun. In the same way, when Mithra's mission on earth was fulfilled, he had been conveyed in the chariot of Helios to the celestial spheres over the ocean, and the happy lot which the hero had won for himself he granted also to his followers. The Emperors in particular were commonly reputed to become companions of the Sun-god after death, as they had been his *protégés* in life, and to be conducted by him in his chariot up to the summit of the eternal vaults.

Finally, there is a very wide-spread belief of Syrian origin that souls fly to heaven on the back of an eagle.[1] According to the story, Etana in Babylon, like Ganymede in Greece, had been carried off in this way. The pious shared this happy lot. This is why the eagle is used as the ordinary decorative *motif* on sepulchral *stelae* at Hierapolis, the holy city of the great Syrian goddess, and it appears with the same meaning in the West. At the funeral rites of Emperors at Rome there was always fastened to the top of the pyre on which the corpse was to be consumed, an eagle, which was supposed to bear aloft the monarch's soul, and art frequently represents the busts of the Cæsars resting on an eagle in the act of taking flight, by way of suggesting their apotheosis. The reason is that in the East the eagle is the bird of the Baals, solar gods, and it carries to its master those who have been his servants in the world below.

All these supposed methods of reaching heaven are very primitive: they start from the supposition that a *load* has to be carried; they hardly imply a separation of body and soul, and they are anterior to the distinctions which philosophers established between different parts of man's being. They are religious survivals of very ancient conceptions, which only vulgar minds still interpreted literally.

The same idea is involved when magicians by secret processes professed to assure the credulous of the possibility of raising themselves upwards. If we are to believe Arnobius,[2] they asserted that they could cause wings to grow from the backs of their dupes, so as to enable them to fly up to the stars. One of the wonders which miracle-mongers most frequently boasted of working was that of soaring up into the air. The phenomena of levitation are produced at all periods. The power which magic professed to bestow on its adepts, is merely one particular application of this art to eschatology or rather to deification (ἀπαθανατισμός). Of this the papyrus erroneously called a "Mithraic liturgy" is the most typical example.[3]

These mechanical means of raising oneself, body and soul,

---

[1] For further details see my paper "L'aigle funéraire des Syriens et l'apothéose des empereurs" (*Revue de l'histoire des religions*), 1910.

[2] Arnob., *Adv. Nat.*, ii, 33, 62 (p. 65, 5; 97, 27, Reifferscheid).

[3] Dieterich, *Eine Mithrasliturgie*, 1910, compare my *Oriental Religions* (1911), p. 260.

to the starry vault could still be recognised by superstition, which picks up all the ideas that have dropped out in the evolution of beliefs. They carry us back to an extremely low stage of religion, as we said. Hence theologians no longer accepted them save as symbols. Other doctrines of a more advanced character were developed, and these constituted the true teaching of the great Oriental mysteries, just as they had secured the adhesion of thinking men. They connected the ascent of the soul after death with physical and ethical theories, and thus caused sidereal immortality to enter into the order of the universe. They either appealed to *solar attraction*, or based their doctrine on the actual *nature of the soul*.

The Pythagoreans already believed that the glittering particles of dust which danced ceaselessly in a sunbeam ($\xi\acute{\upsilon}\sigma\mu\alpha\tau\alpha$), were souls descending from the ether, borne on the wings of light. They added that this beam, passing through the air and through water down to its depths, gave life to all things here below. This idea persisted under the Empire in the theology of the mysteries. Souls descended upon the earth, anp reascended after death toward the sky, thanks to the rays of the sun, which served as the means of transport. On Mithraic bas-reliefs, one of the seven rays which surround the head of *Sol Invictus*, is seen disproportionately prolonged towards the dying Bull in order to awake the new life that is to spring from the death of the cosmogonic animal. But this ancient belief was brought into connection with a general theory held by the Chaldeans.[1] We saw that in the eyes of astrologers the human soul was an igneous essence, of the same nature as the celestial fires. The radiant sun continually caused particles of his resplendent orb to descend into the bodies which he called to life. Conversely, when death has dissolved the elements of which the human being is composed, and the soul has quitted the fleshly envelope in which it was imprisoned, the sun elates it again to himself. Just as his ardent heat causes all material substances to rise from the earth, so it draws to him again the invisible essence that dwells in us. He is the $'A\nu\alpha\gamma\omega\gamma\epsilon\acute{\upsilon}\varsigma$, "he who brings up from below," who attracts the spirit out of the

[1] See above, Lecture IV, p. 73 ss.

flesh that defiles it. By a series of emissions and absorptions he in turn sends his burning emanations into bodies at birth and after death causes them to reascend into his bosom.

In this theory it is to the power of the sun, the great cosmic divinity, that the ascension of the soul is due. According to another doctrine mentioned above, which we are now going to consider more closely, the cause of this ascension is the physical nature of the soul.

This doctrine is set forth with great precision by Cicero in the *Tusculan Disputations*,[1] doubtless after Posidonius. The soul is a fiery breath (*anima inflammata*)—that is to say, its substance is the lightest in this universe composed of four elements. It necessarily, therefore, has a tendency to rise, for it is warmer and more subtle than the gross and dense air which encircles the earth. It will the more easily cleave this heavy atmosphere, since nothing moves more rapidly than a spirit. It must, therefore, in its continuous ascent, pass through that zone of the sky where gather the clouds and the rain, and where rule the winds, which, by reason of exhalations from the earth, is damp and foggy. When finally it reaches the spaces filled by an air that is rarefied and warmed by the sun, it finds elements similar to its own substance, and, ceasing to ascend, it is maintained in equilibrium. Henceforth it dwells in these regions, which are its natural home, continually vivified by the same principles that feed the everlasting fires of the stars.

This theory made it easier than the previous theory had done to establish a firm connexion between ethical beliefs concerning future destiny and physical theories about the constitution of the universe and the nature of man. We have seen[2] that virtue was conceived as liberation from the dominion of the flesh; the soul is never purely spiritual or immaterial, but when it abandons itself to the passions, it becomes gross, its substance grows more corporeal, if I may use the expression, and then it is too heavy to rise to the stars and gain the spheres of light. Its mere density will compel it to float in our mephitic atmosphere until it has been purified and con-

---

[1] *Tusc. Disp.*, i, 43, § 18.
[2] See above, p. 100, and Lecture V, p. 83.

sequently lightened. Thus the door is opened to all doctrines
concerning punishment beyond the grave. How did pagans
conceive this Purgatory situated in the air?

There is a very old opinion that the soul is a breath and that,
at the moment when it escapes through the mouth of the dying
man, it is carried away by the winds. Thus the atmosphere was
filled with wandering souls, which became demons with power
to succour or harm mortals. The origin of these beliefs goes
back to the most primitive animism. But the mysteries introduced into them the idea of purification. Souls tossed by
whirlwinds are freed from defilements contracted during life,
just as linen hung in the air is bleached and loses all odour.
When, after being thus buffeted and blown about by the winds,
souls are purified from part of their sins, they rise to the zone
of the clouds, where they are drenched by rain and plunged
into the gulf of the upper waters. Thus cleansed from the stains
that polluted them, they reach at last the fires of heaven, whose
heat scorches them. Not till they have undergone this threefold
trial, during which they have passed through countless years
of cruel expiation, do they find at length everlasting peace in
the serenity of the ether.

Virgil alludes to this doctrine in the famous line of the sixth
book of the _Æneid_,[1] where, speaking of souls, he says:

> Aliae panduntur inanes
> Suspensae ad ventos, aliis sub gurgite vasto
> Infectum eluitur scelus aut exuritur igni.

Again, the passage of souls through the elements is represented symbolically on a funeral monument almost contemporary with the poet. Above the portrait of the deceased there
appear first in the spandrels of this _cippus_, two busts of the
Winds facing each other. Higher up, on the architrave are two
Tritons and two dolphins, which evidently represent the idea
of the aqueous element. Finally, at the top of the stone, in the
pediment, we see two lions which, as on the Mithraic monuments, are symbols of fire, the igneous principle.[2]

---

[1] Virgil, _Æn._, vi, 740.
[2] _Jahresb. Inst. Wien_, xii (1910), p. 213.

Side by side with physical ideas, mythological beliefs always retained their sway. Various sects professed to assure to the deceased a passage through these regions peopled by malevolent demons: they taught their members prayers which would propïtiate hostile powers; they instructed them in formulæ, consisting of veritable "pass-words," which would compel the commandants (ἄρχοντες), posted to guard the gates of heaven, to allow them to enter the upper sphere. Here is a legacy from the ancient religions of the East. The Egyptian *Book of the Dead* is a veritable guide to the other world, and the Orphic tablets of Petilia are of the same character. The papyrus of Paris, called a Mithraic liturgy, affords us the most characteristic example of the use of these magical processes.

But more often the priests professed to give the soul a god to lead it on its perilous journey through the whirlwinds of air, water, and fire to the starry heavens. "Among the dead," says a funeral inscription,[1] "there are two companies: one moves upon the earth, the other in the ether among the choirs of stars; I belong to the latter, for I have obtained a god as my guide." This divine escort of souls frequently retains the name of Hermes in conformity with ancient Greek mythology. An epigram belonging to the first century of our era apostrophises the deceased in these words: "Hermes of the wingèd feet, taking thee by the hand, has conducted thee to Olympus and made thee to shine among the stars." [2] But more often the rôle of escort now devolves upon the Sun himself: We have seen[3] that at the end of paganism the royal star is figured as carrying mortals in his flying chariot. Those who had not by their piety merited the protection of the god whose duty it was to escort and introduce them, and who nevertheless ventured up to heaven, were cast headlong into the perpetually raging gulf of the warring elements which fought unceasingly around the earth.

---

[1] Kaibel, *Epigramm. Græca*, 650.
[2] Haussoullier, *Revue de philologie*, 1909, p. 6.
[3] See above, p. 101.

3. The lowest of the seven planetary spheres, that of the moon, separates the domain of the violent and restless elements and of beings subject to fate, from that of the eternal gods, where all is order and regularity. What becomes of the souls that enter this celestial zone, and where are they stationed? In other words, *where is the abode of the blest?*—the third question which we have to examine.

The masses did not attain to very precise ideas on this subject: they hesitated, they contented themselves with the general assertion that the soul is "among the stars." At the beginning of their poems, Lucan addressing Nero and Statius addressing Domitian both asked what part of heaven these Emperors will inhabit after their apotheosis [1]: Will they mount on the flaming chariot of the Sun? will they take their place as new stars among the constellations? Or even will Jupiter himself in the height of the heavens yield to them his sceptre? In the same way theologians doubted where to place the Elysian Fields. The Stoics had already emphatically declared that they were not situated in the depths of the earth, as the ancient Greeks believed. In conformity with their system of physical interpretations of mythological names, Acheron became in their eyes the air, Tartarus and Pyriphlegethon the zones of fire and hail. As for the Elysian Fields, they are found to be located sometimes in the moon, sometimes between the moon and the sun, sometimes in the sphere of the fixed stars and particularly in the Milky Way, sometimes beyond this extreme sphere of the heavens, outside the limits of the world. Among the various doctrines there are two of which we have more precise information from ancient authors. One is set forth by Plutarch after Demetrius of Tarsus [2]: it is a combination of the ideas of Posidonius with the religious beliefs of the mysteries. According to this doctrine, man is composed of body ($\sigma\tilde{\omega}\mu\alpha$), nutritive soul ($\psi\nu\chi\acute{\eta}$), and reason ($\nuο\tilde{\nu}\varsigma$). The body is made of earth; the vital principle, which nourishes it and causes it to grow, is lunar; reason comes to us from the sun. Death severs from the body the nutritive soul and the rational soul; the former is

---

[1] Lucan, i, 45 ss. Stat., *Thebaid.*, i, 22
[2] Plut., *De Facie in Orbe Lunae*, c. 26; cf. my *Théologie solaire*, pp. 464, 475.

dissolved in the moon, the latter ultimately, after complete purification, reascends to its original source, the fount of all light.

This doctrine was adopted by those who regarded the Sun as the principal god. But when, as we have explained,[1] paganism renounced the view that the Sun is the lord of the world, the Prime Cause, and set the Supreme Being beyond the limits of the sensible world, enthroning him above the planetary spheres in the highest of the heavens, the abode of the blest was naturally transferred to the seat of divinity; and a theory, more complicated than that of solar immortality, but doubtless only a development of it, prevailed towards the end of the Roman empire.

This psychology, which owed its triumph to the astrological cults of Asia, professed to establish a sevenfold division in the soul, to which corresponded seven creations. It taught that our soul descends from the height of heaven to this sublunary world, passing through the gates of the planetary spheres, and thus at its birth the soul acquires the dispositions and the qualities peculiar to each of these stars. After death it regains its celestial home by the same path. Then, as it traverses the zones of the sky, which are placed one above another, it divests itself of the passions and faculties which it has acquired during its descent to earth, as it were of garments. To the moon it surrenders its vital and alimentary energy, to Mercury its cupidity, to Venus its amorous desires, to the sun its intellectual capacities, to Mars its warlike ardour, to Jupiter its ambitious dreams, to Saturn its slothful tendencies. It is naked, disencumbered of all sensibility, when it reaches the eighth heaven, there to enjoy, as a sublime essence, in the eternal light where live the gods, bliss without end.

All these doctrines, then, in spite of differences in detail, taught that souls, descended from the light above, were raised to the region of the stars, where they dwelt forever with these radiant divinities. This eschatology of "Chaldean" origin gradually displaced all others under the Empire. The Elysian Fields, which not only the ancient Greeks, but also the followers of Isis and Serapis still located in the depths of the earth, were

[1] See above, Lecture IV, p. 75.

transferred to the ether which laves the stars, and the subterranean world became henceforth the gloomy abode of
malevolent spirits. This conception, a novelty in Europe, had
long been that of Persian dualism, which the mysteries of
Mithra imported into the West. Their theology systematically
contrasts the infernal darkness, into which are plunged demons
and reprobates, with the bright abodes of the gods and the elect.

🐍   🐚

4. Before concluding this lecture, we have still a fourth
question to examine: *What conception was formed of the bliss
reserved for the elect who were raised to the stars?*

We have seen (p. 95) that the mysteries of Bacchus and
Thracian Orphism represented immortality as a sort of holy
intoxication: the faithful, sharing the banquet of the gods,
rejoiced with them for ever at a feast liberally supplied with
wine. These beliefs were combined with sidereal eschatology,
only the locality of the repast was transferred to the new
Olympus, and the idea of a celestial banquet was to survive up
to the end of paganism and to impose itself, at any rate as a
symbol, even on Christianity.

But Plato had already ridiculed those who looked upon
ceaseless wine-bibbing as the highest reward of virtue, and the
author of the *Epinomis* already conceived eternal life as the
contemplation of the most beautiful things which eye can perceive—that is, the constellations. This idea was developed in
the sidereal cults, and Posidonius was to set forth in stately
language how the contemplation of the sky and the study of
the stars is the preparation for another existence, in which
human reason will know the fulness of the sublime joy which a
transient ecstasy causes it here below. As soon as it is delivered
from the trammels of the flesh, the soul will soar to these lofty
regions, whither it has hitherto been unable to escape except at
intervals. Flying across the immensity of space, it will reascend
to the stars from which it descended. Embracing in its view the
entire circuit of the world, it will perceive our globe as a
scarcely visible point, or as an ant-heap for the dominion of
which a host of minute insects contend. This earth, frozen in

the north, scorched in the south, submerged all round by the ocean, intersected by deserts, devastated and defiled, is un-inhabitable except here and there. How contemptible will appear to the soul the narrowness of its former dwelling, how empty the ambition of those who dream of no other im-mortality than glory in this finite realm! As soon as it reaches the starry spheres, reason is nourished and expands; in its former home it regains its original qualities; it rejoices among the divine stars; it contemplates all the glory of the bright heaven, and at the same time it is ravished by the accordant sounds of enchanting music, the glorious world-concert made by the harmonious movement of the spheres. Freed from the passions of the body, it will be able to abandon itself entirely to its insatiable desire for knowledge. Marvelling at the sidereal revolutions, it will set itself to comprehend them; its keener vision will enable it to discover the causes of all phenomena, and it will receive a full revelation of all the secrets of Nature—that is, of God.

The doctrine of sidereal immortality is certainly the most elevated that antiquity conceived. It was at this definitive formula that paganism stopped. This belief was not to perish utterly with it; and even after the stars had been despoiled of their divinity, it survived to some extent the theology which had created it. If I had not already abused your patience, it would be an interesting study to join you in searching for survivals of these pagan tenets through the Middle Ages, and in showing the forms which they assumed in the popular creed and amongst the divines. In general, souls continued to be represented as passing through the spheres of heaven in order to reach the abode of the Most High. May I remind you that Dante was still inspired by these most ancient astrological conceptions? His Paradise shows us the blest, who have practised the virtues proper to each of the planets, inhabiting the spheres of these seven wandering stars. To destroy these old eschatological ideas it was necessary for Copernicus and Galileo to overthrow the system of Ptolemy and bring down those heavens peopled by bright beings, and so to open to the imagination the infinite spaces of a boundless universe.

INDEX